Jefferson's Religion

Jefferson's Religion

Stephen J. Vicchio

Wipf & Stock
PUBLISHERS
Eugene, Oregon

11/22/07

FOR
G. 11 t
ROBER-

Dear FR'iads,

TJ [illeglib]

JEFFERSON'S RELIGION

ISBN 13: 978-1-59752-830-6

Cataloging-in-Publication data

Vicchio, Stephen.
Jefferson's Religion / Stephen J. Vicchio

viii + 150 p.; 23 cm.

ISBN 13: 978-1-59752-830-6 (alk. paper)

1. Jefferson, Thomas, 1743–1826. 2. United States—Religion—To 1800.
I. Title.

E332. V53 2007

Manufactured in the U.S.A.

To my wife Sandra,
who began this quest at the dinner table when she asked,
"Did Thomas Jefferson believe in God?"

Contents

Introduction

*When in the course of human events, it becomes necessary for one
people to dissolve the political bonds which have connected them with
another, and to assume among the Powers of the earth, the separate
and equal station to which the Laws of Nature and Nature's God
entitle them, a decent respect to the opinions of mankind requires that
they should declare the causes which impel them to the separation.*

—Thomas Jefferson
    Declaration of Independence

*In matters of religion, I have considered that its free exercise is
placed by the constitution independent of the powers of the general
government. I have therefore undertaken, on no occasion, to prescribe
the religious exercises suited to it but have left them as the constitution
found them, under the direction and discipline of State or Church
authorities acknowledged by the several religious societies.*

—Thomas Jefferson
    Second Inaugural Address
    March 4, 1805

IN ORDER TO understand the genesis of this project on Thomas
Jefferson's religious beliefs, one must know of three separate and connected events. The first of these events was ABC television's broadcast
of President George W. Bush's first Inaugural in January, 2001. During
that broadcast, ABC anchor Peter Jennings made the claim that Thomas
Jefferson was an atheist. At the time, I commented about the remark
to my then colleague, Sister Virginia Geiger, a member of the College
of the Notre Dame philosophy department for over sixty years. Sister
Virginia was also a buff on early American history, particularly the phi-
losophies of the founding fathers, as well as the history of the Carroll
family. Through my conversations with Sister Virginia about the reli-

gions of the founding fathers I was convinced, as she was, that Jefferson was no atheist.

The second item related to the genesis of this book is the death of Sister Virginia, and the fact that I became her literary executor in January of 2003. For over twenty years, Sister Virginia had taught a course on philosophy and the founding fathers. Thus, I inherited the papers of Sister Virginia related to that course. Like most of her other papers and possessions, these papers were very organized and thorough. Her notes on Jefferson, Madison, Washington, and others are scholarly, sophisticated and thorough. A second reason for writing this book, then was the acquisition of these papers.

A third item connected to the genesis of this book is the fact that my wife began working on a project in 2003, in which the Thomas Jefferson Foundation is building a new visitor center at Monticello. My wife Sandra's architectural firm, Ayers Saint Gross, of Baltimore is the architect for this project, and my wife is the project manager.

During my wife's work at Monticello, I have had the pleasure to meet many members of the staff there, as well as the Foundation's board and the Jefferson Library staff. Through research I have done at the Jefferson Library, it became clear to me that Thomas Jefferson was accused of being associated with all sorts of religious persuasions, none of which appeared to be true. In the course of my research, I became convinced that Thomas Jefferson was not an atheist, a deist, a Unitarian, nor, in his adult life, a professed Christian of any denomination. Although Jefferson has been accused of all these things, he appears to have not numbered himself among the members of any of these groups.

This book grew out of these accusations about Jefferson's religion, accusations that existed in Jefferson's day, and continue into contemporary discussions of our third president. Indeed, recently British author Christopher Hitchens, in his book, *Thomas Jefferson: Author of America*, has renewed the "Jefferson as Atheist" mantra; and it appears to be no truer now than it was 200 years ago.

Each of the first four chapters of this book deals with one of the accusations mentioned above. Chapter one with whether Jefferson was an atheist. Chapter two with whether he was a Unitarian. Chapter three with whether our third president was a deist, and chapter four with whether Jefferson thought of himself as a Christian. In the conclusions of all four of these chapters, we argue that Thomas Jefferson was neither atheist, Unitarian, deist, nor Christian.

The final two chapters of this work, chapters five and six, speak more specifically about what Jefferson did not believe about religion, as well as what religious beliefs he did hold. Much of the material for these two chapters is related to Jefferson's two compilations of the four gospels, "A Syllabus of an Estimate of the Merit of the Doctrines of Jesus," and "The Life and Morals of Jesus of Nazareth." In this latter volume, Jefferson cut out of the gospels with a razor what he thought was not the original teachings of Jesus. What Jefferson leaves out, as well as what he leaves in, as we shall see, tells us a great deal about his theological point of view.

Throughout the course of this project, I have acquired a number of debts in its completion. I am deeply thankful for the friendship and encouragement of much of the staff at Monticello and the Jefferson Library. Among these people are Dan Jordan, President of the Thomas Jefferson Foundation; Kat Imhoff, Vice President; Susan Stein, Vice President and Gilder curator; Michael Merrian, Director of Facilities and Construction; Jacque Robertson, Library Director; Bill Bieswanger, a member of the Library staff; and Eleanor Sparagana and Anna Berkes, two other members of the library staff.

I am also indebted to my colleagues at the College of Notre Dame in Baltimore for their constant support and encouragement, particularly our president Mary Pat Seuerkamp, Suzanne Shipley, Vice President for Academic Affairs, Sister Sharon Kanis, my department chairperson, Catriona MacLeod, and Margaret Steinhagen. My life at the college has been, for the most part, a happy and rewarding one. I am grateful for my continued ability to teach here.

I should also acknowledge the support and openness of my publisher, Wipf and Stock, under the direction of K. C. Hanson. K. C. has made this enterprise a painless one—something rare in the book business. I wish also to thank Marissa Larma, who assisted in preparing the index.

I am also thankful to Tryn Lashley who has worked many hours on this manuscript, to my wife Sandra Parsons Vicchio, my partner and dearest friend. And to my two sons Jack and Reed, who continually make my life have its most precious meaning. I also wish to express my gratitude to Maria Wong who helped with the copy editing on this book.

I must also acknowledge the influence of my colleagues and friends in the development of this project, including Charles Ritter, Margaret Steinhagen, Catriona MacLeod, Richard Macksey, Bruce Birch, Tim Craig, Jennifer Boyd, Sara Priebe, Dorothy Brown, and Sisters Therese Marie Dougherty, Theresa Lamy, and Marie Michelle Walsh.

Thomas Jefferson was, without doubt, our most gifted president. He was a philosopher, linguist, scientist, farmer, and loving father and husband. He was also a rare and gifted human being. There is an apocryphal story that when John F. Kennedy invited American Nobel Prize recipients to dinner at the White House, he proposed a toast that went something like this: "Here's to the most brain power ever assembled in this dining room, with the possible exception of when Jefferson dined here alone."

I think Kennedy was right about that. Jefferson was brilliant beyond all but a very few. He was an intelligent and complicated man. His views of religion, as we shall see, are as complicated as his political life. At times these religious beliefs of Jefferson were ambiguous. I hope you enjoy our take on these beliefs.

SJV
Easter Sunday, 2006
Baltimore

Was Thomas Jefferson an Atheist?

There is no proof for that hypothesis.

—Pierre Simon LaPlace (in response to Napoleon's
   objection that LaPlace has omitted God in his
   Celestial Mechanics)

What can be asserted without proof can be dismissed without proof.

—Christopher Hitchens
   "Less Than Miraculous"

*Some have made the love of God the foundation of morality. If we
did a good act merely from the love of God and a belief that it is
pleasing to Him, whence arises the belief of the atheist? Is it idle to
say, as some do, that no such being exists . . . Diderot, D'Alembert,
D'Holbach, Condorcet, are known to have been among the most
virtuous of men. Their virtue, then, must have had some other
foundation than the love of God.*

—Thomas Jefferson
   Letter to Thomas Law (June 13, 1814)

Introduction

IN JANUARY, 2001, during a broadcast of ABC's television coverage
of President George W. Bush's first inaugural, Peter Jennings, the ABC
anchor, made a comment that Thomas Jefferson was an atheist. The comment came in connection with a discussion of Jefferson's religious beliefs,
and the actual comment was "Not many Americans, of course, knew that
Thomas Jefferson was an atheist."[1] This accusation of Mr. Jennings about
our third President was not the first time Jefferson had been called a
non-believer. Indeed, from Jefferson's own time to the present, a number
of thinkers have thought, or accused, Thomas Jefferson of atheism.

In this chapter, we will explore the history of the claim that Thomas Jefferson did not believe in God. We will begin with a section on accusations of Jefferson's atheism in his own time. In a second section in this chapter, we will explore several references to atheism that Jefferson makes in his letters and other writings. In a third section, we will examine some contemporary claims made by journalists that Jefferson was an atheist.

In a concluding section of this chapter, we will supply abundant evidence that Jefferson was not an atheist. Indeed, we will offer substantial proof that the answer to the question posed by the title of this chapter is a resounding No!

Jefferson, Atheism, and His Own Time

Thomas Jefferson in his own time, and for many years after his death, was accused of being an atheist. Many of the attacks on Jefferson's religion had, as their origins, Jefferson's opponents in the election for president of the United States in 1800. Dozens of pamphlets and newspaper articles, in cities along the eastern coast, attacked Jefferson as a "French infidel and atheist."[2] Many sermons were preached in Jefferson's day that if he were elected, he would banish God, overthrow the church, and destroy belief in the Bible as the word of God.[3] Some Jefferson scholars report that prior to the election of 1800, many believers hid their Bibles under mattresses and other places, in the event that Jefferson were to be elected.[4]

The Reverend Thornton Stringfellow, a prominent Virginia divine of Jefferson's day, tells us, "Mr. Jefferson did not bow to the authority of the Bible, and on this subject I do not bow to him." The *International Cyclopedia*, a nineteenth-century American encyclopedia edited by Daniel Coit Gilman, president of Johns Hopkins University, tells us, "In religion it is probable that he [Jefferson] was not far from what was then known and execrated as a Freethinker."

In New England, Rev. John Mason called Jefferson "a confirmed infidel," known for "vilifying the divine word, and preaching insurrection against God."[5] Thomas Robins, a young Connecticut preacher of Jefferson's day, called Jefferson a "howling atheist."[6] Timothy Dwight, the president of Yale in a 1798 speech referred to Jefferson as an atheist.[7] Dwight wrote:

> It cannot be necessary to adopt any train of reasoning to show that a man who disbelieves the inspiration and divine authority of scripture—who not only denies the divinity of our Savour, but reduces him to the grade of an uneducated, ignorant and erring man—who calls the God of Abraham (the Jehovah of the Bible) a cruel and remorseless being, cannot be a Christian.[8]

Timothy Dwight's remarks were typical of New England clergy of the day. The Reverend Bird Wilson, an Episcopal minister and historian, several years after Jefferson's death, wrote, "The founders of our nation were nearly all Infidels."[9] Presumably Thomas Jefferson was one of the people the Rev. Wilson had in mind.

Indeed, among Jefferson's opponents in the election of 1800 none were as fervent as the New England clergy, especially in Connecticut where Congregationalism was the established church. These ministers were solidly biblical in their theology, and solidly Federalist, that is, anti-Jeffersonian, in their politics.

Alexander Hamilton, in his collected published works, called Jefferson an "atheist and fanatic."[10] Daniel Webster, after a visit to Monticello, reported that Jefferson has a preference for "French opinions, morals, and religion."[11] There is no doubt that what Hamilton had in mind was the atheism of Voltaire, the Marquis LaPlace, and others.

In a letter to Mrs. Harrison Smith from August 6, 1816, Jefferson responds to these charges of irreligion made against him by the New England clergy:

> The priests indeed have heretofore thought proper to ascribe to me religious, or rather anti-religious sentiments, of their own fabric, but such as soothed their resentments against the act of Virginia for establishing religious freedom. They wish him to be thought atheist, deist, or devil, who could advocate freedom from their religious dictations.[12]

Again, in discussing infidels, Jefferson suggests that if there were no priests, there would be no infidels:

> My opinion is that there would have never been an infidel, if there
> had never been a priest. The artificial structures they have built on
> the purest of all moral systems, for the moral purpose of deriving
> peace and power, revolt those who speak for themselves, and who
> read in that system only what is really there. These, therefore, they
> brand with such nick-names as their enmity chooses gratuitously
> to impart.[13]

Clearly, Jefferson is referring here to the treatment he has been
given by the clergy. From the election of 1800 to his death, Jefferson
continuously remarks on the clergy, in general, referring to their indict-
ment of Jefferson's atheism, or, that the clergy themselves have missed
the genuinely true doctrines of religion.

In a letter to John Adams from July 5, 1814, Jefferson refers to the
Christian clergy:

> The Christian priesthood, finding the doctrines of Christ leveled
> to every understanding, and too plain to need explanation, saw in
> the mysticism of Plato materials with which they might build up
> an artificial system, which might from its indistinctness, admit
> everlasting controversy, give employment for their order and in-
> troduce it to profit, power, and preeminence.[14]

In this letter, and in many others as well, Jefferson suggests that
Plato was the origins of much of traditional Christian doctrine, or, if
not Plato, then the early church fathers' interpretation of Plato's metaphysics. In another letter written to Charles Thompson on January 9,
1816, Jefferson again refers to the connection of Plato's thought to early
Christianity:

> I am a real Christian, that is to say, a disciple of the doctrines
> of Jesus, very different from Platonists, who call me infidel and
> themselves Christians.[15]

In countless other letters, Jefferson disparages both Plato and
the Christian clergy. He saves particular scorn for Calvin and the
Presbyterians, and generally believes that the doctrines of Jesus were
corrupted by the history of early Christianity and its clergy. Richard
Hildreth, noted historian and writer on Jefferson tells us:

Jefferson seems to have considered himself excessively ill-treated by the clergy, who were constantly twitting him with his infidel opinions.[16]

Indeed, throughout Jefferson's work, the President suggests that the Christianity of his contemporary clergy did not include the beliefs of Jesus, but rather the teachings of Plato, including his emphasis on immortality of the soul. In a letter to Thomas Law, in discussing defections from this Platonic Christianity, Jefferson observes:

> I have observed, indeed, generally, that while in Protestant countries the defection from the Platonic Christianity of the priest is to Deism, in Catholic countries they are to Atheism.[17]

Jefferson goes on in the same letter to mention a number of French atheists, so it is likely that the country he had in mind was France.[18]

The other source of claims that Jefferson was an atheist was the Federalist Party, that ran a candidate against Jefferson in the election of 1800. The Federalists, and their followers, produced a number of broadsides against Jefferson prior to the election. John Fenno in the *Federalist Gazette of the United States* wrote, "The excessive patriots of Paris . . . appear to be in the same cast with the enemies of the constitution of this country."[19] "We are not Frenchmen," wrote a Connecticut writer, "and until Atheistical Philosophy of a certain Virginian shall become the fashion (which God of his mercy forbid) we shall never be."[20]

One of the sources for the Federalists' critique of Jefferson's religion was a line that came from Jefferson's *Notes on Virginia*. When asked about his religious belief, Jefferson wrote, "It does me no injury for my neighbor to say there are twenty gods or no gods. It neither picks my pocket, nor breaks my leg."[21] The Federalist clergy of New England seized on the remark as proof positive that Jefferson was some stripe of infidel, pagan, or heretic. Sermons in the pulpit and editorials in newspapers throughout New England played on the theme that the greatest religious country in the world was now ruled by a man who did not believe in the central doctrines espoused by Christianity.

A Rev. Dr. Wilson, in his essay, "The Religion of the Presidents," suggests Jefferson was an infidel:

I believe the influence of his example and name has done more for the extension of infidelity than that of any man. Since his death, and the publication of Randolph (his works edited by his grandson), there remains not a shadow of doubt of his infidel principles. If any man thinks there is, let him look at the book itself. I do not recommend the purchase of it to any man, for it is one of the most wicked and dangerous books extent.[22]

The Rev. John S. C. Abbot in his *Lives of the Presidents* made the same claim about Jefferson's infidelity.[23]

Other members of the press also were no less kind to Jefferson. *The New American Cyclopedia* in its 1860 edition tells us that "Jefferson discarded faith as unphilosophical, he became an Infidel."This statement was seen by some as offensive, so the 1874 edition reported:

He carried the rule of subjecting everything to the test of abstract reason into matters of religion, venerating the characters of Christ, but refusing belief in his divine mission.[24]

The New York Observer, after the publication of Jefferson's works by his grandson, remarked:

Mr. Jefferson, it is well known, was never suspected of being very friendly to the orthodox religion, but these volumes prove not only that he was a disbeliever, but a scoffer of the lowest class.[25]

The *Chicago Tribune*, commenting on Jefferson's religion at the close of the nineteenth century, said this:

A question has been raised about Mr. Jefferson's religious views. There need be no questions, for he has settled that himself. He was an infidel, or, as he chose to call it, a Materialist. By his own account he was as heterodox as Colonel Ingersoll, and in some respects more so.[26]

The reference to Ingersoll is Robert Green Ingersoll (1833–1899), a noted American orator and lawyer, who professed atheism and agnosticism in his lectures and writings.

The *Connecticut Courant* in Jefferson's day suggested that the President

Opposed everything sacred,[27]

And that if Jefferson and his

> Democrats could acquire control of our religious establishments ...
> They would destroy them.[28]

In Saul K. Padover's biography of Jefferson, he describes the sentiments of the New England clerical Federalists:

> The religious issue was dragged out, and stirred up flames of hatred
> and intolerance. Clergymen, mobilizing their heaviest artillery of
> thunder and brimstone, threatened Christians with all manner of
> dire consequences if they should vote for the "infidel" [Jefferson]
> from Virginia. This was particularly true in New England, where
> the clergy stood like Gibraltar against Jefferson.[29]

William Linn in a New York pamphlet prior to the 1800 election wrote of Jefferson's "disbelief in the Holy Scriptures."[30] Linn said he made this conclusion "culled principally from his own writings."[31]

The pamphlet was entitled, "Serious Considerations on the Election of a President." Linn, a Dutch Reform minister, accuses Jefferson of "heinous crimes of not believing in revelation," and a plan to "introduce immorality," into the American scene. He called Jefferson a "true infidel," and insisted that "an infidel like Jefferson could not, should not, be elected."[32]

Linn concluded this pamphlet with this appeal for "Christians to defeat the infidel from Virginia:

> Will you, then, my fellow citizens, with all this evidence . . . vote
> for Mr. Jefferson? . . . As to myself, were Mr. Jefferson connected
> with me by the nearest ties of blood, and did I owe him a thou-
> sand obligations, I would not, and could not vote for him. No;
> sooner than stretch forth my hand to place him at the head of the
> nation. "Let mine arms fall from shoulder blade, and mine arm
> be broken from the bone."[33]

Even after Jefferson's death in 1826, rumors persisted about Jefferson that he was a non-believer. As late as 1830, public libraries in Philadelphia banned books on Jefferson from their shelves.[34] George Bancroft (1800–1891), American statesman and historian, comments on Thomas Jefferson's religion in his *History of the United States*:

He was not only a hater of priest craft and superstition and big-
otry and intolerance; he was thought to be indifferent to religion.[35]

Jefferson's character and faith were called into question in both the
presidential elections of 1796 and 1800. In 1796, he was accused of being
an atheist and a Jacobin. Prior to 1800, Jefferson was attacked for atheism, cowardice, personal immorality, and with cohabitating with Sally
Hemings.[36] But in all these accusations, nowhere in Jefferson's writings,
either his letters or his other published writings, did he say that he was
a non-believer.

Jefferson, Atheism, and Contemporary America

In addition to the comment by Peter Jennings in the opening of this
chapter, more recently, Christopher Hitchens, a British-born writer for
Vanity Fair, has revived the "Jefferson as Atheist" mantra. In his book,
Thomas Jefferson: Author of America, in several recent articles, and in a
number of speeches, Hitchens has repeated the Jefferson as atheist
claim.

In *Thomas Jefferson: Author of America*, Hitchens comments:

Jefferson more than once wrote to friends that he faced the ap-
proaching end without either hope or fear. This was much to say
that, in the most unmistakable terms, that he was not a Christian.
As to whether he was an atheist, we must reserve judgment if
only because of the prudence he was compelled to observe during
his political life.[37]

In another section of *Thomas Jefferson: Author of America*, Hitchens
is even more explicit about Jefferson's religion. At the time of his death
Jefferson "was not a Christian, and may have been an atheist."[38]

In a letter from Hitchens to Lenni Brenner, a contemporary
American historian of the Revolutionary Period, in which Brenner had
requested evidence for Hitchens' claim that Jefferson was an atheist,
Hitchens wrote:

It can't be proved that he was an atheist but it can be argued (A
distinction in my book that you ignore). He wrote several times
that he faced extinction without "hope or fear," which certainly

means he was not a Christian. No man of any cloth was asked to his well-anticipated deathbed, and his headstone/obelisk more or less speaks for itself.[39]

We will discuss Jefferson's obelisk in a later section of this chapter, but Hitchens seems here to suggest that it is evidence that Jefferson was an atheist. In a number of recent speeches and articles, Hitchens also makes the claim about Jefferson's atheism. In a June 16, 2005, speech on Jefferson at the 92nd Street Y in New York City, for example, Hitchens described Jefferson as an atheist during the question period that followed his lecture.[40] Similar claims were made in a number of other lectures, as well.

In another speech given in Arlington, Virginia, for example, on June 17, 2005, during the question and answer period that followed Hitchens' talk on *Thomas Jefferson: Author of America,* the journalist was asked about Jefferson's religious beliefs. Hitchens responded, "I don't think he had any."[41] In a third speech about his book *Thomas Jefferson: Author of America*, given at the Monticello Speakers Forum on September 14, 2004, Christopher Hitchens also said, "I suspect that Thomas Jefferson was an atheist."

We will respond to Hitchens claims about Jefferson's obelisk, as well as his view that Jefferson was an atheist in the final sections of this chapter. It is enough now, however, to point out that several times in public Hitchens has proclaimed himself to be a nonbeliever, like a recent interview when Hitchens said, "I'm an atheist. I'm not just neutral about religion, I'm hostile to it. I think it is a positively bad idea, not just a false one."[42]

In an article for the *Nation,* Hitchens suggests that Mother Theresa is "a dangerous, sinister person who properly belongs in the caboose of the Pat Buchanan baggage train."[43] In addition to raising doubts about Mother Theresa, Christopher Hitchens has written about religion in a number of other contexts. Not only is Hitchens' view of Jefferson's religion colored by his own atheism, he seems to express disdain for any form of religious devotion.

But before we respond to Hitchens' claim that Jefferson was an atheist, we shall look first at several places in Jefferson's works, where our third president mentions or discusses atheists and/or atheism.

Jefferson on Atheism

In a letter to John Adams, written on April 11, 1823, Jefferson discusses John Calvin, the chief proponent of the Reformed movement in sixteenth-century Europe, Jefferson says this:

> I can never join Calvin in addressing his god. He was indeed an Atheist, which I can never be; or rather his religion was Daemonism. If ever man worshipped a false God, he did. The being described in his 5 points is not the God whom you and I acknowledge and adore, the Creator and benevolent governor of the world.[44]

In a letter to Richard Price from Paris on January 8, 1789, Jefferson wrote:

> I concur with you strictly in your opinion of the comparative merits of Atheism and Demonism, and really see nothing but the latter in the being worshipped by many who think themselves Christians.[45]

Later in the same letter to John Adams from April 11, 1823, Jefferson writes:

> Every Christian sect gives a great handle to Atheism by their general dogma that, without a revelation, there would not be sufficient proof of the being of God.[46]

Jefferson mentions atheism and atheists in many of his letters, but he does not claim in any of them that he is one of them. Indeed, Jefferson seems to do just the opposite. Rather than seeing himself as an atheist, Jefferson frequently accuses others of atheism—and when he mentions it in his letters, it is always in a pejorative manner.

In a letter to his nephew, Peter Carr, on advice about going to college, Jefferson advises his nephew:

> Fix reason firmly in her seat, and call to her tribunal every fact, every opinion. Question with boldness even the existence of a god; because, if there be one, he must approve the homage of reason rather than blind-folded fear.[47]

Later, in the same letter, Jefferson continues:

If it ends in a belief that there is no god, you will find incitements to virtue in the comfort and pleasantness in its exercise and in the love of others it will procure for you.[48]

In this letter, Thomas Jefferson tells his nephew to question the existence of God. He also suggests that if his nephew concludes there is no God, that he might find his happiness in virtue; but nowhere in this letter, or any of his other epistles, does Jefferson say that he is an atheist. He appears to acknowledge in this letter, and elsewhere, that there are atheists in his day, but he never claims to be among their ranks.

In letters to John Adams on April 8, 1816 and April 11, 1823, Jefferson refers to these atheists of his day:

... Both [atheist and theists] agreed in the order of the existing system [nature of the universe], but the one supposed it from eternity, the other as having begun in time. (April 8, 1816) [49]

The argument which they [atheists] rest on as triumphant and unanswerable is that in every hypothesis of cosmogony, you must admit an eternal pre-existence of something. (April 11, 1823) [50]

Jefferson goes on to suggest that the atheists of his day believed that the universe had no beginning and no end, while genuine Christians of his day believed that the universe was created by God out of nothing. But it is instructive to notice that when Jefferson speaks here of atheism, it is in the third person, and nowhere in the entire corpus of Jefferson's writings does he claim to be an atheist. Nowhere does Jefferson discuss atheism in the first person.

In a letter to Albert Gallatin on June 16, 1817, in discussing a move by the Pennsylvania state legislature to require belief in God a necessary qualification for office, Jefferson points out that the bill was defeated, "although assuredly there was not a single atheist in the body."[51] Jefferson continuously refers to atheists in his own day in a number of his other letters, but it is always in the third person.[52]

In writing to extend his bill of religious freedom in Virginia, Jefferson suggests that this right should extend to "the Jew, and the Gentile, the Christian and Mahometan, the Hindoo, and the infidel of every denomination."[53] This seems to imply that Jefferson thought there were infidels in every religious persuasion, but nowhere does he claim to be among them.

In a letter to John Adams dated August 15, 1820, while discussing what he called "Immaterialism," Jefferson commented:

> At what age of the Christian church this heresy of immaterialism, this masked atheism, crept in, I do not know. But a heresy it certainly is. Jesus taught nothing of it.[54]

In these comments, it is clear that Jefferson believed there were atheists of his day, and that the Immaterialists were among them, but Jefferson does not say that he belonged to either group.

Response to Contemporary Claims of Jefferson's Atheism

Christopher Hitchens, contemporary critic of Jefferson's belief in God, rests his conclusion on several pieces of evidence. First, Jefferson's obelisk mentioned earlier. Second a number of letters in which Jefferson at the end of his life says he is "without hope and fear." Third, these letters imply, Hitchens argues, that [this] "means that Jefferson was not a Christian."[55] And fourth, Hitchens points out that no man of the cloth was asked to Jefferson's "well-anticipated deathbed."[56]

It is best to take each of these pieces of evidence one at a time. Let us begin with Jefferson's obelisk. In 1826, just before his death, Jefferson wrote a note on his epitaph:

> On the face of the Obelisk the following inscription, and not a word more
>
> Here was buried Thomas Jefferson
>
> Author of the Declaration of American Independence of the Statute of Virginia for religious freedom and Father of University of Virginia
>
> Because by these, as testimonials that I have lived, I wish most to be remembered.[57]

It goes without saying that there is no evidence here that Thomas Jefferson was a proponent of atheism. In fact, the grave marker seems to endorse religious belief, with Jefferson's mention of religious freedom.

Thus, it is not entirely clear why Hitchens believes that Jefferson's obelisk is evidence for the President's atheism. Hitchens says the obelisk speaks for itself, but it is not entirely clear what the journalist thinks the obelisk says.

The second bit of evidence—that Jefferson's letters suggest he is "without hope and fear" at the end of his life—is no less convincing.

In none of Mr. Jefferson's letters have we found the expression that our third president was in the face of death "without hope and fear." The closest we may come to this expression is a letter by Jefferson written on March 14, 1820. In that letter, Jefferson wrote:

> Were it necessary however to form an opinion, I confess I should, with Mr. Locke, prefer swallowing one incomprehensibility rather than two. It requires one effort only to admit the single incomprehensibility of matter endowed with thought: and two to believe, 1st that of an existence called Spirit, of which we have neither evidence nor idea, and then secondly, how that spirit which has neither extension nor solidity, can put material organs into motion. These are things that you and I may perhaps know ere long. We have so lived as to fear neither horn of the dilemma. We have, willingly, done injury to no man; and have done for our country the good which has fallen in our way, so far as commensurate with the faculties given us. That we have not done more than we could cannot be imputed to us as a crime to any tribunal. I look therefore to that crisis, as I am sure you also do, as one *"qui summum nec metuit diem nec optat."*[58]

Jefferson's Latin can be translated as "Who neither fears the final days, nor hopes for it." This letter is as close as Jefferson's corpus gets to "without hope and fear." But again, what we have here is hardly proof for atheism.

Hitchens' claim that Jefferson being "without hope and fear" in the face of death, is evidence that Jefferson was not a Christian. Yet, in a number of letters, Jefferson seems to have concluded just the opposite. In a letter to Charles Thompson dated January 9, 1816, for example, Jefferson writes:

> I am a real Christian, that is to say, a disciple of the doctrines of Jesus, very different from the Platonists who call me infidel and themselves Christians and preachers of the gospel, while they

draw all their Dogmas from what its Author never said nor saw. They have compounded from the heathen mysteries a system beyond comprehension of man, of which the great Reformer of the vicious ethics and deism of the Jews, were He to return on earth, would not recognize no any feature.[59]

In a letter to Benjamin Rush dated April 21, 1803, Jefferson again refers to his relationship to Christianity:

To the corruptions of Christianity I am, indeed, opposed; but not the genuine precepts of Jesus himself. I am a Christian, in the only sense in which He wished any one to be, sincerely attached to his doctrines, in preference to all others.[60]

In the same letter to Charles Thompson from January 9, 1816, Jefferson says, "I am a Christian, that is to say, a disciple of the doctrines of Jesus."[61]

If Thomas Jefferson were not a Christian, it certainly raises a number of questions about why he called himself one. In a letter to August Woodward on March 24, 1824, Jefferson refers to "Jesus Himself, the Founder of our religion."[62] Jefferson was a follower of Jesus, particularly his moral teachings, as evidenced by this letter to William Canby from September 18, 1813:

Of all the systems of morality, ancient or modern, which have come under my observation, none appears to be so pure as that of Jesus. He who follows this steadily need not, I think, be uneasy, although he cannot comprehend the subtleties and mysteries erected on his doctrines.[63]

In a letter to William Short from August 4, 1820, Jefferson suggests he reveres Jesus as the greatest moral teacher in history. He admired Jesus as the preeminent reformer of the Jewish religion whose extraordinary moral sense enabled him to enunciate universally valid truths. In Jefferson's judgment, Jesus was "the Herald of truths reformatory of mankind in general, but more immediately that of his own countrymen . . . ."[64]

Again, if Christopher Hitchens is correct about Jefferson not being a Christian, then why did the president seem so enamored with the moral teachings of Jesus? Saying that Thomas Jefferson was not a believer in God, and in the Christian faith, seems to fly in the face of many of Jefferson's own words.

As to Hitchens' claim that Jefferson did not reveal his atheism because of political effects, in a letter written to Dr. Benjamin Waterhouse on June 26, 1822, it is clear that Jefferson no longer had any worries about his political reputation, four years before his death.

This leaves us with Hitchens' fourth bit of evidence—that no member of the clergy was present at his deathbed. Although this appears to be true, it could be pointed out that the Episcopal clergy presided at Jefferson's baptism, and his first communion, as well as at the death of his wife Martha in 1782 at the age of 33. If Jefferson did not believe in God, then why was there Episcopal clergy officiating at that burial, as well as the burials of the four children of Martha Jefferson's that did not survive.

There is also the evidence of Jefferson's funeral as well. Sanford points out that a member of the Episcopal clergy presided at Jefferson's funeral.[65] There were also Episcopal clergy at the funerals of Martha Jefferson and their four children who died early in life. Hitchens may be correct that there were not clergy present at Jefferson's death bed, but there were at his funeral, and the funerals of his family members as well.

Henry Stephens Randall tells us that the only people at Jefferson's death bed were his grandson, Thomas Jefferson Randolph, his granddaughter's husband, Nicholas Trist, his physician, Dr. Robley Dunglison, and some servants (specifically mentioned is his butler, Burwell Colbert).[66]

The only account of Thomas Jefferson's final days comes from the account of his grandson, Thomas Jefferson Randolph. Randolph tells us:

> Upon being suddenly aroused from sleep, by a noise in the room, he asked if he has heard the name of Mr. Hatch—the minister whose church he attended. On my replying in the negative, he observed, as he turned over, "I have no objection to see him, as a kind and good neighbor."[67]

Randolph goes on to offer an interpretation of what his grandfather meant:

> The impression made upon my mind at the moment was, that his religious opinions having been formed upon mature study and reflection, he had no doubts upon his mind, and therefore did not desire the clergyman; I have never since doubted the correctness of the impression then taken.[68]

Perhaps Randolph's conclusion about his grandfather's remark is the best interpretation, but could it not also mean that he wanted Mr. Hatch at his deathbed? Jefferson did not say he did not want Mr. Hatch. He said if he were to be there, he would accept him as a good and kind neighbor. Thus, Christopher Hitchens is correct that no minister was present at Thomas Jefferson's deathbed.

Randall goes on to say that Rev. Hatch did preside at Jefferson's funeral. Randall remarks, "The day was rainy, or the crowd would have been greater. The burial service of the Episcopal Church was read over Mr. Jefferson's remains by his friend, the Rev. Mr. Hatch, the clergyman of the parish . . ."[69]

There is no evidence one way or the other about clergy being present at the deaths of Jefferson's children. There is, however, reference to the funeral of Mary Jefferson Epps, one of his granddaughters. In a note on the Memorandum Books about Mary Jefferson Epps' funeral, it reads:

> MJE died at Monticello from complications incident to the birth of her third child on 15 Feb. [1804]. The Rev. Matthew Maury officiated at her burial in the Monticello graveyard.[70]

Further Evidence That Jefferson Was No Atheist

The most important evidence that Jefferson was not an atheist were his own words. Hundreds of times in his letters, Jefferson assents to his belief in God. Jefferson writing to Benjamin Waterhouse wrote that "there is only one God, and He is all-perfect."[71] In another letter to Waterhouse dated January 8, 1825, Jefferson claimed he was "anxious to see the doctrine of one God commenced in our state."[72] In a dispute with his friend, Miles King, Jefferson refers to God as the "final arbiter of truth."[73] Writing to John Adams on April 11, 1823, Jefferson refers to "the God whom you and I adore."[74] Jefferson repeatedly referred to God in his letters. Indeed, there are at least 100 mentions in those letters that Jefferson believed in God.

In a reply to a group of Baptists Jefferson wrote in 1807:

> Among the most inestimable of our blessings is that ... of liberty to worship our Creator in the way we see most agreeable to His will.[75]

In a letter to Miles King in September 26, 1814, in connection with a discussion of religion, Jefferson wrote, "Our particular principles of religion are a subject of accountability to God alone."[76] In a letter to Benjamin Rush on September 23, 1800, Jefferson wrote, "I have sworn upon the altar of God, eternal hostility against any form of tyranny over the mind of man."[77] In a letter to John Adams from January 11, 1817, while discussing his religious beliefs Jefferson wrote, "Say nothing of my religion. It is known to my God and myself alone."[78] In all these examples, and in countless others in his letters, Jefferson regularly proclaimed a belief in God.

In a letter to Mrs. John Adams on January 11, 1823, Jefferson refers to "the Being that presides over the world who is essentially benevolent."[79] In a letter to Benjamin Waring from March 23, 1801, Jefferson tells his friend, "I offer my sincere prayers to the Supreme Ruler of the universe ..."[80]

In addition to evidence from his letters, there is also a good bit of evidence for Jefferson's belief in God in his published works. When writing the *Rights of British America*, in 1774, Jefferson remarked, "I tremble for my country when I reflect that God is just; that His justice cannot sleep forever."[81] In another passage in the *Notes on Virginia*, Jefferson wrote:

> Can the liberties of a nation be thought secure when we have removed their only fireballs, a conviction in the minds of people that these liberties are of the gift of God? That they are not to be violated but with His wrath.[82]

Jefferson begins his *Act For Establishing Religious Freedom*, proposed in the Virginia State Assembly in 1786 this way:

> Well aware that Almighty God hath created the mind free; that all attempts to influence it by temporal punishments or burthens,

or by civil incapacitations, tend only to beget habits of hypocrisy and meanness, and are a departure from the plan of the Holy Author of our religion, who being Lord both of body and mind, yet chose not to propagate it by coercions on either, as was in his Almighty power to do.[83]

Even the opening of the *Declaration of Independence* gives evidence of Jefferson's belief in God:

We hold these Truths to be self-evident, that all Men are created Equal, that they are endowed by their Creator with certain Inalienable Rights . . . [84]

And in both of his inaugural addresses, President Jefferson refers to God. In the first address from March 4, 1801, Jefferson mentions "an adoring and over-ruling Providence," and the "Infinite Power which rules the destinies of the universe."[85] In his second inaugural address, Jefferson alludes to "needing the favor of that Being, in whose hands we reside."[86]

In addition to all this evidence, there are also the numerous mentions of scripture that Thomas Jefferson makes in his writings. Many of them are like this quotation from Psalm 18:9–10, where Jefferson writes:

The Lord descended from above, and bowed the heavens most high and underneath His feet, he cast the darkness of the sky.[87]

In countless other passages in his letters, as well as his other writings, Jefferson quotes scripture; and the passages he chooses frequently imply his belief in the deity.

This evidence suggests that not only did Thomas Jefferson believe in God, he also thought that God answers prayers, guides the universe, and rules the universe with a powerful benevolence. It also suggests that Jefferson held these views at the time of his inaugurals in the early part of the nineteenth century, as well as in letters shortly before his death.

Daniel J. Boorstin, in his book, *The Lost Worlds of Thomas Jefferson*, speaks of Jefferson's view of God as Author of Nature. Boorstin writes:

Jefferson on more than one occasion declared "the eternal pre-existence of God and His creation of the world" to be the foundation of his philosophy.[88]

Boorstin goes on to point out that many eighteenth-century thinkers held the view that the universe is eternal and thus was uncreated. Boorstin adds:

> But Jefferson emphatically rejected any such hypothesis; the earth must have been a solid from its first creation, and the Creator must, at the outset, have given its present shape to insure a perfect equilibrium.[89]

On many occasions in his letters our third president makes the claim that if there is a God, and he believed there was, He must have made it possible to human beings to discover His existence and His character. Jefferson believed that those who say the story of creation could not be known unless visible facts were supplemented by Christian revelation, were actually giving a handle to atheism—some that Jefferson was staunchly against.

Conclusions

We began this chapter by raising the question, "Was Thomas Jefferson an Atheist?" We began to answer this question by exploring Jefferson's contemporaries and their accusations that Jefferson was an atheist. In Jefferson's time, those accusations came from three principal sources: the clergy of New England who often saw Jefferson as a non-believer; the popular press in Jefferson's day, particularly those publications associated with the Federalists; the third source is members of the Federalist Party who were intent on keeping Jefferson out of the White House after the election of 1800.

In a second section of this chapter, we have explored claims made by two contemporary journalists that Jefferson was an atheist. Both Peter Jennings and Christopher Hitchens have held or hold the belief that our third president was a non-believer.

In a third section of this chapter, we discussed several places in Jefferson's writings where he speaks or writes about atheism. In this third section, we made two major conclusions: that Jefferson always spoke of atheism in the third person; and that Jefferson did not consider himself to be an atheist.

In the fourth section of this chapter, we responded to the claims of Jennings and Hitchens. Among Hitchens' claims were these four: 1) Jefferson's grave marker suggests his atheism; 2) at the end of his life, Jefferson wrote that he was "without hope and fear." 3) Jefferson did not speak of his non-belief in God for political reasons; and finally, no member of the clergy was present at his death bed. In the fourth section of this chapter, we have responded to all these claims, finding them all to be spurious.

In the final section of this first chapter, we provided ample evidence that Jefferson was not an atheist, and that he believed in God. This evidence came principally from Jefferson's letters, comments he made on religion in his published works, as well as Jefferson's many uses of scripture throughout his writings. The bottom line in this chapter should be quite clear: Jefferson Was No Atheist!

In the second chapter of this work, we take up another question about Jefferson's religious point of view: "Was Thomas Jefferson a Unitarian?" As we shall see, the answer to this query is both yes and no.

Notes

1. Peter Jennings, ABC television coverage of George W. Bush's First Inaugural. January 20, 2001.

2. R. B. Bernstein, *Jefferson* (New York: Oxford University Press, 2003.) 81–104; Edwin S. Gaustad, *Sword on the Altar of God* (Grand Rapids: Eerdmans, 1996) 89–94.

3. Gilbert Chinard, *Thomas Jefferson: The Apostle of Americanism* (Ann Arbor: University of Michigan Press, 1996.) 367–73.

4. Ibid., 389.

5. John Mason cited in Phillip Hamburger, *Separation of Church and State* (Cambridge: Harvard University Press, 2002) 115.

6. Ibid.

7. Timothy Dwight, *A Discourse on Some Events of the Last Century Delivered In the Brick Church in New Haven on Wednesday, January 7th, 1801* (New Haven, 1801) 27.

8. Ibid., 28.

9. Reverend Doctor Bird Wilson, sermon delivered in October, 1831. Quoted in John E. Remsburg's *Six Historic Americans*. (New York: 1906) 1. Also quoted in Paul F. Boller, *George Washing and Religion* (Dallas: Southern Methodist University Press, 1963) 14–15.

10. Alexander Hamilton letter to John Jay, May 7, 1800, in *The Works of Alexander Hamilton*, edited by Henry C. Lodge (New York, 1904) Volume 10, 372–73.

11. Charles Sanford, *The Religious Life of Thomas Jefferson* (Charlottesville: University of Virginia Press, 1984) 1–2.

12. Jefferson to Mrs. Harrison Smith, August 6, 1816.

13. Jefferson to John Adams, July 5, 1814.

14. Jefferson to John Adams, July 5, 1814.

15. Jefferson to Charles Thompson, January 9, 1816.

16. Richard Hildreth, *History of the United States* (New York: Scholars Press, 1972) Volume V, 461.

17. Jefferson to Thomas Law, June 13, 1814.

18. Ibid.

19. Bernstein, 96.

20. Hamburger, 116.

21. Thomas Jefferson, *Notes on Virginia*, 1781.

22. Rev. Dr. Wilson quoted in Franklin Steiner, *The Religious Beliefs of Our Presidents* (New York: Haldeman-Julius, 1936) 169.

23. John S.C. Abbot, *Lives of the Presidents* (Portland, Maine: Hallett and Company, 1890) 67.

24. *The New American Encyclopedia* (1874) Volume 3, 183.

25. *The New York Observer* quoted in Hamburger, 117.

26. *Chicago Tribune,* quoted in Hamburger, 117.

27. *Connecticut Courant* quoted in Hamburger, 118.

28. Ibid.

29. Saul K. Padover, *Jefferson: A Great American's Life and Ideas* (New York: Mentor Books, 1964) 116.

30. William Linn, quoted in Steiner, 171.

31. Ibid.

32. Saul K. Padover, *Jefferson: A Great American's Life and Ideas* (New York: Mentor Books, 1964) 117.

33. Ibid.

34. Sanford, 2.

35. George Bancroft, *History of the United States* (1834) Volume I, 17.

36. See Joseph Ellis' *American Sphinx* (New York: Vintage Books, 1996) 363–67.

37. Christopher Hitchens, *Thomas Jefferson: Author of America* (New York: Harper Collins, 2005) 28.

38. Ibid.

39. Lenni Brenner, "Jefferson, Hitchens, and Atheism," in *Counterpunch* (July 26, 2005).

40. Christopher Hitchens, Lecture on *Thomas Jefferson: Author of America* (New York City, 92nd Street YMCA, June 16, 2005).

41. Christopher Hitchens, Speech in Arlington, Virginia, January 17, 2005.

42. Ibid.

43. Christopher Hitchens, "The Ghoul of Calcutta," in *For the Sake of Argument* (New York, Verso Books, 1993).

44. Jefferson to John Adams, April 11, 1823.

45. Jefferson to Richard Price, January 8, 1789.

46. Letter to John Adams, April 11, 1823.

47. Jefferson to Peter Carr, August 19, 1785.

48. Ibid.

49. Jefferson to John Adams, April 8, 1816.

50. Jefferson to John Adams, April 11, 1823.

51. Jefferson to Albert Gallatin, June 16, 1817.

52. See Jefferson to Richard Price, January 8, 1789; and Jefferson to John Adams, April 11, 1823, for examples.

53. Thomas Jefferson, *Autobiography* (1821).

54. Jefferson to John Adams, August 15, 1820.

55. Hitchens, p. 28.

56. Ibid.

57. Thomas Jefferson's burial site, Monticello, Virginia.

58. Jefferson to Benjamin Rush, March 14, 1820.

59. Jefferson to Charles Thompson, January 9, 1816.

60. Jefferson to Benjamin Rush, April 21, 1803.

61. Jefferson to Charles Thompson, January 9, 1816.

62. Jefferson to August Woodward, Marcy 24, 1824.

63. Jefferson to William Canby, September 18, 1813.

64. Jefferson to William Short, August 4, 1820.

65. Charles B. Sanford, *The Religious Life of Thomas Jefferson* (Charlottsville: University of Virginia Press, 1984) 4–5.

66. Henry Stephens Randall, *The Life of Thomas Jefferson* (New York: Derby and Jackson, 1858) Volume III, 543.

67. Ibid.

68. Ibid.

69. Ibid., 545.

70. Personal communication from Anna Berkes, Jefferson Library Reference Desk, April 6, 2006.

71. Jefferson to Benjamin Waterhouse.

72. Jefferson to Benjamin Waterhouse, January 8, 1825.

73. Jefferson to Miles King, September 26, 1814.

74. Sanford, 11.

75. Jefferson reply to Danbury Baptist, January 2, 1802.

76. Jefferson to Miles King, September 26, 1814.

77. Jefferson to Benjamin Rush, September 23, 1800.

78. Jefferson to John Adams, January 11, 1817.

79. Jefferson to Mrs. John Adams, January 11, 1823.

80. Jefferson to Benjamin Waring, Mach 23, 1801.

81. Thomas Jefferson, *Rights of British America* (1774).

82. Thomas Jefferson, *Notes on Virginia* (1782).

83. Thomas Jefferson, *Notes on the State of Virginia* (Chapel Hill: University of North Carolina Press, 1954) 223.

84. Thomas Jefferson, *Declaration of Independence* (1776).

85. First Inaugural Address, March 4, 1801.

86. Second Inaugural Address, March 5, 1805.

87. Jefferson to John Adams, October 13, 1813. In addition to this quotation from the Psalms, Jefferson also quotes from Genesis, Ecclesiastes, Job, Joshua, Psalms, the four gospels, Paul's letters, and the book of Revelation.

88. Daniel J. Boorstin, *The Lost World of Thomas Jefferson* (Chicago: University of Chicago Press, 1993) 30.

89. Ibid.

Was Thomas Jefferson a Unitarian?

Lord Viscount Bolingbroke gave Jefferson his heterodox views on Religion, which "emphasized a deistic, universal, impartial God of natural religion whom Jefferson referred to in the Declaration of Independence as 'Nature's God.'

—Allen Jayne
  Jefferson's Declaration of Independence:
  Origin, Philosophy, and Theology (1998)

I trust there is not a young man now living in the United States who will not die a Unitarian.

—Thomas Jefferson
  Letter to Benjamin Waterhouse (June 26, 1822)

'Priestly was the English champion of Unitarianism, who became one of Jefferson's friends after moving to the United States in 1794, to escape political persecution in his own land, argued that Christianity was originally a simple religion that had been corrupted by the early church in a misguided effort to make it intellectually respectable . . .

—Eugene Sheridan
  Jefferson and Religion

Introduction

IN THIS CHAPTER, we hope to explore the issue that resides in its title. We will attempt to go about answering this question in several parts. First, what does it mean to say someone is a Unitarian, and, more importantly, what did it mean for one to say he was a Unitarian in Jefferson's day?

A second task taken up in this chapter is to look carefully at the origins and history of Unitarianism, in the hope of asking and answering our first question mentioned above. In a third section of this chapter, we shall carefully look at places in the public record where Thomas Jefferson spoke or wrote about the Unitarians. In a final section of this chapter, we shall make a judgment that the proper answer to the question that stands at the head of this chapter is yes, and no.

The Origins of Unitarianism

The origins of the ancient heresy, sometimes called "Anti-Trinitarianism," are to be found in the Arian controversy of the early fourth century. Arius (256–336) was a presbyter of Alexandria who challenged Bishop Alexander of Alexandria on the issue of God's nature. The dispute lasted from 318–381, and it required the meetings of 18 councils before it was resolved.

The Arian heresy began with the Council of Nicaea in 325, and ended with the Council of Constantinople in 381. The subject of the dispute was the meaning of the Incarnation in relation to the Christian premise of monotheism. Arians like Arius, Praxeas, Sabellius, and others had viewed Christ as virtually a transient manifestation of God; Arius thought he had detected this view in a charge to his clergy on the part of Alexander, bishop of Alexandria.

Arius made a sharp distinction between the Father and the Son, subordinating the latter to the former. This set the stage for the controversy; the subtle distinction between "homoousian" and "homoiousian" became the center of the dispute. Is the Son (homoousias) with the Father (of the same essence or substance), or is he homoiousias, (of a similar essence or substance)? The Nicene formula, holding that the Father and Son, are of the same substance, became the orthodox view, beginning in 325.

Among the arguments that the Arians used against the Trinity were several New Testament passages that they believed were proof texts against the view that Jesus was divine. Among these passages were John 17:3, John 8:42, and Galatians 4:14. In the first of these, the Arians argued, it is implied that there is only one true God. John 8:42 suggests that Jesus "proceedith forth," and thus indicates that Jesus was created. In the passage from Galatians, "You receive me as an angel of God, as Christ Jesus himself," the Arians suggest, implies that Jesus is an angel, and thus not a participator in the Godhead.

After the time of Arius, the Arian party was led by Eusebius of Nicomedia, a fellow pupil of Arius, along with Lucian, who remained under cover but attempted to court intrigue and slander against the leaders of the Nicene party. From 334 to 361, because of the favor of Constantius, the second son of Constantine and an Arian, the Arian view was given relatively free reign. It is during this period that three distinct schools of Arianism arose: the strict Arians or Anomoians, the Semi-Arians, or Homoiousian Party, and the Homoians.

The first of these groups asserted the unlikeness of Christ to the Father. The second confirmed the "of being" or "of likeness" identity of the Son to the Father. The third group held an intermediate view on the issue of substance and being.

In 362, at a Council presided over by Athanasius, the Semi-Arians and Nicenes gradually grew together, and the way was paved for the condemnation of Arianism. The Council of Nicaea was called by the Emperor Constantine in 325 to enable the church to speak with a single voice on matters of faith. The main business of the council was determining a position on the relationship of Christ to God, the Father. The Trinitarian formula was introduced, and the position of the Alexandrians was successfully argued by Saint Athanasius.

The principal product to come out of the council was the Nicene Creed. Athanasius generally is held responsible for the wording of the creed that fixed some of these dogmatic issues. The wording of Athansius' creed looks like this:

> We believe in one God, the Father Almighty, Creator of heaven and earth, and of all things visible and invisible.

> And in one Lord Jesus Christ, the only-begotten Son of God, begotten of the Father before all worlds, God of God, light of light, true God of true God, Begotten not made, being of one substance with the Father by whom all things were made; who for us men, and for our salvation, came down from heaven, and was incarnated by the Holy Spirit of the Virgin Mary, and was made man, and was crucified also for us under Pontius Pilate. He suffered and was buried, and on the third day he rose again according to the scriptures, and ascended into heaven, and sittith at the right hand of the Father. And he shall come again with

glory to judge the living and the dead, whose kingdom shall have no end.

And we believe in the Holy Spirit, the Lord and Giver of life, who proceeds from the Father and Son, who with the Father and Son together is adored and glorified, who spoke by the prophets. And we believe in one holy, Catholic and apostolic church. We acknowledge one baptism for the remission of sins. And we look for the resurrection of the dead, and the end of the world to come. Amen.[1]

Athanasius is generally held responsible for the Christian doctrine of the Trinity. As we shall see later in the chapter, Thomas Jefferson believes that Athanasius is responsible for a good bit of the corruption of the doctrines of Jesus, which, he believes, did not contain a doctrine of the Trinity.

The subsequent history of Arianism was largely confined to its missionary efforts among Germanic tribes. In this connection the name Ulfilas (311–383), called the "Apostle to the Goths," and translator of the biblical text into the Gothic language, is the most notable figure.

Ulfilas converted many of the Visogoths and Ostrogoths to an Arian form of Christianity. An extant letter by Ulfilas' foster son and pupil, Auxentuis of Durostorum, suggests the Arian beliefs of Ulfilas' day. The letter is owned by the University of Uppsala Library in Sweden. Auxentius gives this account of his creed:

I believe that there is only one God the Father, alone unbegotten and invisible. And in His only-begotten Son, our Lord and God, creator and maker of all things, not having any like unto Him. Therefore, there is one God to all, who is also God or our God. And I believe in one Holy Spirit, an enlightening and sanctified power. As Christ says after the resurrection to his apostles, "Behold I send the promise my Father upon you; but tarry in the city of Jerusalem until you are clothed with power from on high." (Luke 24:49) And again: "You shall receive power coming upon you by the Holy Spirit." (Acts 1:8) Neither God nor Lord, but the faithful minister of Christ; not equal, but subject and obedient in all things to the son. And I believe the Son to be subject and obedient to the Father in all things.[2]

Arianism became a kind of natural creed for Germanic tribes in the Dark Ages. At various times in the sixth century, Italy was Arian under the Ostrogoths. Spain was Arian under the Visogoths, and much of North Africa was Arian under the Vandals. Arianism was wiped out during the reign of Justinian, and through the Lombards, it was brought back to Italy in the late sixth century. Traces of the heresy remain in the west until the Muslim conquest in the eighth century.

Unitarianism in the Modern World

From its inception in Transylvania in the middle of the sixteenth century, Unitarianism has been a movement that asserts there is only one God, God the Father, rather than three persons in one God, as the traditional doctrine of the Trinity holds. Unitarians believe in God, but they do not believe in the divine nature of Jesus, nor in the Holy Spirit as an embodiment of the Godhead. In Jefferson's time, what it meant to be a Unitarian was the description given above. A Unitarian was one who denied the Trinity, as well as the human nature of Jesus, while holding to the doctrine of what Unitarians called, "the unity of God."

Modern Unitarianism is usually dated to the period of the Protestant Reformation. A Unitarian movement began in Transylvania in the 1560s. The leader of this group was Francis David (1510–1576). The Unitarians prospered in Poland as a minor Reformed Movement until persecutions forced its members into exile around 1660.

David originally had trained as a Catholic priest, before becoming a Lutheran and then a Calvinist. In 1568 Hungarian King John Sigismond called a Diet in the city of Turda, to determine which of the established religions would be declared the official religion of his realm. During the debate Francis David held his ground against the other established religions in the region. David attempted to convince the King to declare Unitarianism the state religion. Instead, the King made a proclamation of religious freedom and toleration, the first such known declaration in European history. A few years later, King John had died, and his successor did not hold his tolerant views. Francis David was ultimately sentenced to prison for refusing to acknowledge that Christ was to be adored. He died in prison in 1579.

Two other key figures in early Modern Unitarianism were Laelius Socinus (1525–1562) and Faustus Socinus (1539–1604). These two Italian reformers, an uncle and nephew, were the leaders of the religious movement known as Socianism. The Socians established a college at Racov, where the Racovian Catechism of 1605 was developed by Socinus' followers. The Catechism rejected the trinitarianism of the Nicene Creed, as well as the divinity of Jesus. In 1638, the center at Racov was broken up, and by 1658, it was suppressed in Poland.

In addition to these Polish sixteenth-century Unitarians, Michael Servetus (1511–1553), a Spaniard martyred in the Reformation, was also an early European Unitarian. Servetus criticized the doctrine of the Trinity and the use of infant baptism. In 1531, Servetus published his *De Trinitatis Erroribus, On the Errors of the Trinity*. In the following year, Servetus published a second volume on the Trinity, *Dialogorum de Trinitate, (Dialogues on the Trinity)*. A short time later, Servetus' books were confiscated, and he was banned from several Protestant towns, mostly for his denial of the Trinity.

By the publication of Servetus' magnum opus, *Christianismi Restitutio (The Restitution of Christianity)* Servetus was declared an anathema all over Western Europe, and all but three copies of the *Restitution* were destroyed. In the *Restitution*, Servetus denied belief in original sin, the atonement, and the dual natures of Jesus, as well as the doctrine of the Trinity.

Modern Unitarians in England and America thought of Servetus as one of their own. They considered him one of the early constructors of the Unitarian theological movement. Those followers of Servetus and the Polish Racovians who went into exile often settled in East Prussia and Holland. From Holland, Unitarianism spread to England. Isolated Unitarians existed in Britain in the seventeenth century. Most notable of these was John Biddle (1615–1662), who was repeatedly imprisoned for his anti-Trinitarian views. John Biddle is known as the father of English Unitarians.

Later English Unitarians included Joseph Priestly (1773–1804), the discoverer of oxygen, as well as a variety of experiments on a number of gases. Priestly is important for our purposes because he was a friend of Thomas Jefferson, and a number of the letters between them are extant.

Unitarians came to America as early as 1710, and by 1750, most of the Congregational ministers in and around Boston had ceased to regard the doctrine of the Trinity as an essential Christian doctrine. In America, then, the religious liberalism that came to be known as Unitarianism began in the Congregational churches of Massachusetts, as a reaction to the revivalism of the New Awakening (1740–1743). The election of Henry Ware as Hollis Professor of Divinity at Harvard University touched off a controversy, as the result of which the Unitarians became a separate denomination. In 1788, King's Chapel was the first Anglican church in New England to declare itself Unitarian, when its rector, with the consent of his congregation, deleted from the liturgy any mentions of the Trinity. The transformation of Unitarians in New England Congregationalism seemed complete with the appointment of Henry Ware to the Hollis Chair of Divinity at the Harvard Divinity School in 1805.

In 1815, Calvinist Jedidiah Morse reprinted in his magazine, *The Panoplist,* a chapter from a British Unitarian, Thomas Belsham's *Life of Theophilus Lindsey*, published in 1812. Theophilus Lindsey (1723–1808) was educated at St. John's, Cambridge. He was one of the earliest of modern English Unitarians. His *Conversations Upon Christian Idolatry*, published in 1792, as well as his earlier work, *An Historical View of the State of Unitarian Doctrine* (1783), were two important contributions to early modern Unitarian doctrine.

Morse included his own commentary as a preface to this work. In the book, Morse suggested that American liberal ministers dishonestly disguised their true theology and were, in fact, full-fledged Unitarians.

William Ellery Channing was one of the leaders of the liberal wing of the New England Congregationalists. Channing's sermon, "Unitarian Christianity," which was delivered in 1819 at the ordination of Jared Sparks, provides a good description of American Unitarian beliefs of Jefferson's time. Channing's sermon was delivered on May 5, 1819 at what was then called The First Independent Church of Baltimore, which later became the First Unitarian Church of Baltimore.

In this sermon, Channing gives an extensive treatment to those things Unitarians of the day believed in, and those things which Unitarians of Jefferson's time rejected. Among the items Channing says Unitarians believed in were: the authority of the Bible; the use of reason to understand the Bible; the unity of God; and the moral perfection of God.

By the "unity of God" Channing says

That there is only God, and one only ... This proposition seems exceedingly plain we understand by it, that there is one being, one mind, one person, one intelligent agent, and only one, to whom underived and infinite perfection and dominion belong.[3]

Among the propositions that Channing and other Unitarians of his day disavowed were: the Trinity; the dual natures of Jesus; the atonement; and original sin. About the Trinity, Channing said this:

We object to the doctrine of the Trinity, that whilst acknowledging in words it subverts in effects, the unity of God. According to this doctrine, there are three infinite and equal persons, possessing supreme divinity, called the Father, Son, and Holy Ghost. Each of these three persons has his own particular consciousness, will, and perceptions. They love each other, converse with each other, and delight in each other's society. They perform different parts in man's redemption, each having his own appropriate office, and neither doing the work of the other.[4]

Later Channing concludes:

We do, then, with all earnestness, though without reproaching our brethren, protest against this irrational and unscriptural doctrine of the Trinity.[5]

In 1838, Ralph Waldo Emerson's (another Unitarian) divinity school address declared that religious truth should be based on the authority of the inner conscience, not on external historical proofs. The address was given at the Harvard Divinity School on the evening of July 15, 1838. Emerson had been chosen by the senior class to deliver the address.

As the nineteenth century progressed, Unitarianism became more liberal and radical. Emerson and other Unitarian leaders like Theodore Parker (1810–1860) rejected what remaining metaphysical elements there were in the sect's belief system.

In addition to Emerson's speech at the Harvard Divinity School, other manifestoes of Unitarian beliefs existed among their leaders. Theodore

Parker's *A Discourse of the Transient and Permanent in Christianity* (1841) is a fine example. In this work, Parker denied the Trinity, and the dual natures of Jesus, while assenting to the more permanent elements of Jesus' moral point of view.[6]

Emerson shared Jefferson's concern that "historical Christianity" had muddied the message of its founder. But whereas Jefferson worked to retrieve the ethical teachings of Jesus, Emerson mined the gospels for something far more elusive—"the mystery of the soul." Standing before the small group of Divinity School graduates, Emerson called for the young ministers to renounce preaching the "tropes" of the gospels, and to point their congregations back to their "Divine natures."

The problem with the established church, Emerson argued, is that it teaches our smallness instead of our largeness. "In how many church-es," he asked, "by how many prophets, tell me, is man made sensible that he is an infinite soul; that the earth and heavens are passing into his mind; that he is drinking forever the soul of God?" Emerson replaced American Puritanism with Transcendentalism, and substituted the indi-vidual's concern for his soul for the church's concern with sin.

Thomas Jefferson shared the Transcendentalist's concern with the soul; but Emerson did not deny Jesus' divinity as Jefferson did; he simply said that the same potential resides in every human heart.

The Unitarians of the early nineteenth century also gave rise to an important philosophical and literary movement known as Transcendentalism. Indeed, it began as a reform movement of the Unitarian Church. Transcendentalists sought to extend the views of William Ellery Channing about an in-dwelling God, and the impor-tance of intuition in religious belief. Among the proponents of American Transcendentalism were Charles Mayo Ellis, Ralph Waldo Emerson, Amos Bronson Alcott, Margaret Fuller, and Henry David Thoreau.[7]

The Boston Transcendentalists also were influenced by Swedish philosopher, mystic, and anti-trinitarian thinker, Emanuel Swedenborg (1688–1772). In his *Arcana Caelestia* (1749–1756), and in *The True Christian Religion*, published at the end of his life, Swedenborg wrote sev-eral essays denouncing the doctrine of the Trinity.[8] Swedenborg's tracts against the Trinity were a great influence on a number of modern think-ers. Immanuel Kant wrote an entire work, *Traeume des Geistersehers*, refut-ing Swedenborg.[9] Johann August Ernesti, one of the great eighteenth-century German biblical scholars, spent some time and energy refuting Swedenborg's exegetical methods.[10]

More specifically, Swedenborg was a great influence on Balzac, Baudelaire, William Blake, Yeats, and Strindberg. Among the Boston Unitarians, Swedenborg's theological points of view influenced the thinking of Emerson, William Ellery Channing, Benjamin Fisk Barrett, and Henry James Sr., the father of William and Henry James.[11]

More critical and conservative Unitarians of the day were critical of Emerson's speech and Parker's work, as well as their followers, who came to be known as the Transcendentalists. Some within the ranks of Unitarians thought it prudent to remain aligned with traditional Christianity, while others found Christianity to be intellectually limited and emotionally restrictive. Finally, in 1961, the Unitarians merged with the Universalists in the Unitarian Universalist Association, two denominations with parallel histories and beliefs.

From this analysis and history, it should be clear that the Unitarians of Jefferson's day, for the most part, denied the Trinity and the dual natures of Jesus. And it was these two claims that lay at the heart of the movement. We shall now move to a third section of this chapter where Thomas Jefferson mentions or discusses the Unitarians in his works.

Jefferson on the Unitarians

Thomas Jefferson makes a number of references to Unitarianism and Unitarians is his letters and published works. In a letter to William Canby, dated September 18, 1813, Jefferson refers in a pejorative way to

> The demonstration of St. Athanasius, that three are one, and one is three; and yet that the one is not three, nor the three one.[12]

In another letter to Benjamin Waterhouse from June 26, 1822, Jefferson again refers to St. Athanasius:

> I expect it would be but a sermon to the wind. You will find it as difficult to inculcate these sanative precepts on the sensualities of the present day, as to convince an Athanasian that there is but one God.[13]

Jefferson goes on in this letter to describe what he believed to be the doctrines of Jesus (including belief in one God) with the dogmas of John Calvin, which Jefferson says involved "that there are three Gods."[14]

In a letter written to Francis Adrian Van der Kemp on July 30, 1816, Jefferson again ridicules the doctrine of the Trinity:

> Ridicule is the only weapon which can be used against unintelligible propositions. Ideas must be distinct before reason can act upon them; and no man ever had a distinct idea of the Trinity. It is the mere Abracadabra of the mountebanks calling themselves the priests of Jesus.[15]

In another letter written to Jared Sparks on November 4, 1820, Jefferson again speaks of the Trinitarian formula of Athanasius. "The metaphysical insanities of Athanasius of Loyola, and of Calvin, are, to my understanding, mere lapses into polytheism, differing from paganism only by being more unintelligible."[16]

In a letter to Thomas Cooper written on November 2, 1822, Jefferson discusses the role that Unitarianism had begun to play in New England. Jefferson says

> In Boston, however, and its neighborhood, Unitarianism has advanced to so great strength, as now to humble this haughtiest of all religious sects; in so much that they condescend to interchange with them and the other sects, the civilities of preaching freely and frequently in each other's meeting houses. In Rhode Island, on the other hand, no sectarian preacher will permit a Unitarian to pollute his desk.[17]

For the most part, when Thomas Jefferson mentions Unitarianism or Unitarians it is in a positive light. He recognized it was a growing religious faith of his day, he admired the Unitarian faith in some of his friends, and in one particular letter, he seems to come very close to suggesting that he was to be numbered among the ranks of the Unitarians. The letter in question has been used as an epigram to this chapter.

In one section of the letter, Jefferson refers to the Unitarians:

> Be this the wisdom of Unitarians, this the holy mantle which shall cover within its charitable circumference all who believe in one God, and who love their neighbor![18]

But in another section of the same letter, Jefferson writes, "I trust there is not a young man now living in the United States who will not die a Unitarian."[19]

I think what Jefferson meant by this comment is several things. First, he had some serious doubts about the Trinity and the dual natures of Jesus. When we discuss Jefferson's beliefs in the final chapter of this work, we will say more about these doubts. Secondly, he thought these particular ideas of traditional Christianity were outmoded and at times were being rejected by many in his day. And finally, that Jefferson is a great admirer of people who were willing to stand up and assent to a belief against these ideas. Among those in this third category was Joseph Priestly, a man that Jefferson admired for his Unitarian beliefs. It is to Priestly, and his relationship to Jefferson, we wish to turn in the next section of this section.

These first few conclusions are borne out by another letter Jefferson sent to Dr. Waterhouse, another Unitarian, on January 8, 1825. Jefferson comments:

> I am anxious to see the doctrine of one God commenced in our state. But the population of my neighborhood is too slender, and is too much divided into other sects to maintain any one preacher well. I must therefore be contented to be an Unitarian myself, although I know there are many around me who would become so, if once they could hear the question fairly stated.[20]

Again, Jefferson seems to be assenting to a belief in one God, while backing off assenting to the Trinity or the dual natures of Jesus. Jefferson also seems to be saying that many people around him, if properly given the alternatives, would consent to his beliefs as well.

Similarly, in a letter written to J. P. P. Derieux on July 25, 1788, Jefferson talks about his lack of belief in the Trinity. Jefferson says, "My difficulties of reconciling the ideas of Unity and Trinity have persisted from a very early part of my life."[21] Jefferson's *Notes on Heresy* reveal other instances when Jefferson was worried about the relation of the Father to the Son. Jefferson translated the ancient commentaries of Irenaeus, Origen, and Eusebius. His conclusion: a belief in a consubstantial Trinity was contrary to early Christian thought.[22]

In a letter to James Smith, Jefferson also refers to the Trinity:

> The hocus pocus phantasm of a God, like another Cerberus with
> one body and three heads, had its birth and growth in the blood
> of thousands and thousands of martyrs.[23]

Thomas Jefferson mentions the Trinity and Unitarians in a number of his letters. He always saw the former in a negative way, and the latter in a positive way. For Jefferson, what it meant to be a Unitarian was a belief in one God, and a concomitant denial of the Trinity and the dual natures of Jesus.

Joseph Priestly's Influence on Jefferson

The influence of English scientist Joseph Priestly on the religious beliefs of Thomas Jefferson can not be overestimated. Priestly's *Corruptions of Christianity*, published in 1782, was a kind of metaphysical Bible for Jefferson. In the book, Priestly argued that the true teachings of Jesus were obscured and obfuscated by the early church. As the early church fathers adapted Christianity to the Mediterranean world, they contrived doctrines altogether foreign to biblical thought and the teachings of Jesus.

Chief among these doctrines, in Priestly's view, were the Trinity, the dual names of Jesus, the incarnation, and original sin. Priestly believed that a reform of the Christian doctrines was in order, where it would be purged of all Greek influences and doctrinal absurdities.

Jefferson was so impressed with the *Corruption of Christianity* that in a letter to John Adams on August 22, 1813, he specifically mentions Priestly, and another man, Conyers Middleton, an English Deist, as his metaphysical underpinnings. Jefferson wrote, "I rest on them . . . as the basis of my own faith."[24]

Thomas Jefferson refers to Priestly being the source of the President's view that the early teachings of Christianity had been circumvented. Jefferson writes:

> The establishment of the innocent and genuine character of this
> benevolent Moralist [Jesus] and the rescuing it from the impu-
> tation of imposture, which had resulted from artificial systems,
> invented by ultra-Christian sects, unauthorized by a single word
> ever uttered by Him, is a most desirable object, and one to which
> Priestly has successfully devoted his labors and learning.[25]

It is clear that Jefferson was fond of Priestly, and of the Unitarians as well, and that he knew the works of various Unitarians, when he comments in a letter to Timothy Pickering on February 27, 1821:

> As the Creator has made no two faces alike, so no two minds, and probably no two creeds. We well know that among the Unitarians themselves there are strong shades of difference, as between Doctors Price and Priestly, for example. So there may be peculiarities in your creed and in mine.[26]

Jefferson knew Priestly's views well, and respected deeply his views in particular about the Christian religion.

Eugene Sheridan, writing about the influence of Priestly on Jefferson remarks:

> Priestly, a noted English chemist and Unitarian theologian, set forth a highly demythologized version of Christianity which so impressed Jefferson that he adopted key parts of it and later described the work itself as "the groundwork of my view of the subject," and as "one of the basis of my own faith."[27]

Jefferson, in a letter to Priestly on the latter's arrival in America, speaks of the President's compatibility with the views of the English scientist:

> Those who live by mystery and charlatanerie, fearing you [Dr. Priestly] would render them useless by simplifying the Christian philosophy—the most sublime and benevolent but most perverted system that ever shone on man—endeavored to crush your well-earned and well-deserved fame.[28]

Later in the same letter, Jefferson welcomes Priestly to America:

> It is with heartfelt satisfaction that, in the first moments of my public action, I can hail you with welcome to our land, tender to you the homage of its respect and esteem, cover you under the protection of those laws which were made for the wise and good like you, and disdain the legitimacy of the libel on legislation.[29]

Jefferson deeply respected Joseph Priestly and frequently counted on his advice in matters of state, in his views on Christianity and religious toleration, as well as on the curriculum at the University of Virginia.

This letter came as a response to an attempt by Timothy Pickering, Secretary of State, an avid Federalist, to have Priestly deported under the 1799 Alien Act. Priestly was not deported because of the scientist's friendship with President Adams. Andrew Burstein speaks of the event:

> Jefferson read Priestly's *History of the Corruptions of Christianity* (1782) in the early or mid 1790s, and a short time later had the pleasure of welcoming its author to American shores, as a political refugee. Priestly shared Jefferson's hope for the ultimate success of the French Revolution, and had suffered in his homeland for his unpopular stand, his papers and scientific equipment incinerated at the hands of an angry mob. In exile in Pennsylvania, he so publicly embraced Jefferson's politics that Secretary of State Timothy Pickering, a Federalist diehard, urged Priestly's deportation under the 1799 Alien Act. He was spared, because President Adams esteemed him. As a practical, scientific, liberal republican religious thinker, Joseph Priestly believed himself born into "a most wonderful an important aera in the history of mankind."[30]

From Priestly, Jefferson inherited many of his ideas on Jesus and the religion he founded. To quote Burstein again:

> He [Priestly] undertook his work on Christianity, he claimed, from a devotion to "the discovery and communication of truth." The Jesus he found in his research did not claim any special powers, and the apostles as well did not consider him more than "a man approved by God, by signs and wonders which God did by him."[31]

Priestly presented to Jefferson what he formerly referred to as "rational Christianity," and Jefferson adopted this view that was consistent with long-standing Unitarian beliefs.

Priestly's books made a deep and lasting impression on Jefferson. As Sheridan continues:

> It convinced him that the early Christians had a Unitarian conception of God and that therefore one like himself could be a true Christian without being a Trinitarian. It convinced him that Jesus never laid claim to divinity, which to him made Jesus more credible as a great moral teacher. It increased his appreciation of

Christian morality by demonstrating to his satisfaction that the dogmas that led him to reject the validity of Christianity in his youth were in fact perversions of the primitive Christian message rather than integral parts of it.[32]

Jefferson accepted Priestly's conviction that Christianity was a simple religion whose original emphasis on the unity of God and the primacy of morality over dogma had been corrupted by the history of Christian theology. Sometimes Jefferson attributes these corruptions to the Christian clergy, and at other times to the machinations of Greek philosophy.

More books of Priestly's followed. *Letters to a Philosophical Unbeliever* (1774); *Disquisitions Relating to Matter and Spirit* (1777); *The History of the Corruptions of Christianity* (1782); and *History of Early Opinions Concerning Jesus Christ* (1786), all continued his Unitarian themes to deny the Trinity, Jesus' divinity, and other Christian doctrines. In *The History Concerning Early Opinions on Jesus*, Priestly defended Unitarianism and attacked such Christian doctrines as the inspiration of scripture, the Virgin Birth, the Trinity, and the Atonement.

British reactions to these books were scathing. Priestly was called an atheist. Goaded by Tory politicians, Priestly's home and chapel were burned down by a Birmingham mob in 1791. After moving to France and, as the French Revolution took a turn for the worse, Priestly immigrated to the United States in 1794. He settled with his family in Northumberland, Pennsylvania.

Priestly quickly made friends with a number of American politicians, including Thomas Jefferson. Jefferson acquired from Joseph Priestly features of his metaphysical world view, which he found confirmed for the rest of his life. These include a disdain for Platonic and Neo-Platonic metaphysics; a fierce loathing of all priest craft whose practitioners he held guilty of perpetuating superstitions in the name of Jesus for centuries.

Priestly and Jefferson carried on a correspondence from 1800 to 1804. In January 1800, Jefferson wrote to Priestly to inquire if the scientist would assist him in constructing a curriculum for the new University of Virginia. In a follow-up letter from January 27, 1800, Jefferson included some remarks about the teaching of languages in the new university, something he left out of the earlier letter.

Writing from Washington two months after his inauguration, Jefferson sent a letter to Priestly vilifying those who "live by mystery and charlataneria." Speaking of their shared metaphysical point of view, Jefferson told Priestly:

> We can no longer say there is nothing new under the sun. For this whole chapter in the history of man is new. The great extent of our Republic is new. Its sparse habitation is new. The mighty wave of public opinion, which has rolled over it is new.[33]

In another letter written from Washington to Priestly from April 9, 1803, Jefferson comments on a copy of Priestly's *Socrates and Jesus* sent to him by Benjamin Rush. Jefferson was delighted with the book, and saw it as an inspiration to begin a work that would chart Jefferson's view of Jesus. Jefferson points out that he had promised Rush in 1798–99 that he would write something to sketch out his views of the Christian religion and its founder. Twelve days later on April 21, 1803, Jefferson sent his *A Syllabus on The Morals of Jesus* to Rush, as well as a copy to Priestly.

In another letter written in Washington to Priestly, dated January 29, 1804, Jefferson commends Priestly for the latter's desire to compare the teachings of Jesus with some of the ancient Greek philosophers. Jefferson comments:

> I rejoice that you have undertaken the task of comparing the moral doctrines of Jesus with those of the ancient philosophers. You are so much in possession of the whole subject, that you will do it easier and better than any other person living.[34]

In this letter, Jefferson also tells Priestly he has sent for copies of the gospels in Greek, French, and Latin, from a Philadelphia book dealer, so that he might paste into a blank book the portions of the evangelists he did not excise with a razor. This text, with the gospels in four columns (Greek, Latin, French, and English) became the *Syllabus*. More is said about this text in chapter five of this work, but it is enough to say now that Jefferson removed from the gospels those lines he believed were not original.

Jefferson respected Joseph Priestly as a scientist and as a theologian. On countless occasions, Jefferson writes about his sympathy with Priestly's metaphysics. More than any other figure, Priestly influenced Jefferson's views of religion in the latter part of the President's life. Like Priestly, Jefferson considered Jesus a teacher of a sublime and flawless ethic. Writing to the Unitarian physician, Benjamin Rush, Jefferson said:

> To the corruption of Christianity, I am indeed opposed; but not to the general precepts of Jesus himself. I am a Christian, in the only sense he wished any one to be; sincerely attached to his doctrines, in preference to all others; ascribing to himself all human excellence, and believing he never claimed any other.[35]

Jefferson found the Unitarian understanding of Jesus compatible with his own. In 1822, he predicted that "there is not now a young man living in the United States who will not die a Unitarian." Jefferson requested that a Unitarian minister be dispatched to his area of Virginia:

> Missionaries from Cambridge [that is, Harvard Divinity School] would soon be greeted with more welcome, than from the tritheistical school of Andover.[36]

Jefferson is referring here to Andover Divinity School, which was founded near Boston in 1807. Today it is known as the Andover-Newton School of Theology. Jefferson suggests that a Unitarian minister would be more welcome to Virginia than a Presbyterian or Anglican clergyman who believes in the Trinity.

Thomas Jefferson never joined the Unitarian Church. He did attend Unitarian services while visiting Priestly in Pennsylvania, and he spoke highly of those services. He corresponded on religious matters with numerous Unitarians, among them Jared Sparks (Unitarian minister, historian, and president of Harvard University), Thomas Cooper, Benjamin Waterhouse, Benjamin Rush, John Adams, and Joseph Priestly.

Jefferson was perhaps most open about his own religious beliefs in his long correspondence with John Adams, during his late years, 1812–1826. In these letters, Jefferson and Adams shared their belief in what Priestly and others had called "the unity of God." They also shared a disdain for a number of traditional Christian doctrines, including the Trinity, the dual natures of Jesus, original sin, and the atonement.

Typical of these letters is this disparagement of Plato by Jefferson in a letter to Adams on July 5, 1814:

> I amused myself with reading seriously Plato's Republic. I am wrong however in calling it amusement, for it was the heaviest task-work I ever went through.[37]

Later in the same letter, Jefferson labels Plato as a sophist, and places at his feet responsibility, along with the Christian clergy, for the corruption of the doctrines of Jesus.[38] In another letter to Adams in which Jefferson discusses Plato and other Greek philosophers, Jefferson comments

> We must dismiss the Platonists and Plotinists, the Stagyrites and Gamalielites, the Eclectics, the Gnostics and the Scholastics, their essences and emanations, their Logos and Demiurgos, Aeons and Daemons, male and female, with a long train of etc. etc. etc., or, shall I say at once, of Nonsense.[39]

In these letters to Adams at the end of his life, Jefferson affirms his beliefs in Unitarian ideas, while at the same time disdains the view that Greek philosophy made any real contributions to the history of the Christian faith. Indeed, Jefferson saw Plato and others as the inventors of ideas that corrupted the faith of Jesus. Plato and the priests corrupted the doctrines of Jesus by introducing to the Judeo-Christian tradition, ideas foreign to the Old Testament like resurrection, immortality, and belief in Satan as a demonic force. Jefferson believed that these ideas, and others like the atonement, the divinity of Jesus, and original sin, were concepts that arose in the early history of the Christian church—ideas that were foreign to Jesus as well.

The Influence of Other Unitarians on Jefferson

In addition to the influence that Joseph Priestly had on Thomas Jefferson other members of the Unitarian faith also had an influence on our third president. Chief among these other influences was Benjamin Rush. Rush (1746–1813) was a physician, teacher, and friend of Thomas Jefferson.

Benjamin Rush and Thomas Jefferson carried on an extensive correspondence, often having the topics of these letters turn to matters of religion. Rush may have been responsible for Jefferson's denial of original sin. Rush was against the idea that evil could be explained as the intrusion of an external Satanic force on a pure human nature. As Rush put it, "Physical and moral evil began together."

Daniel Boorstin describes Benjamin Rush's view:

> Once man has been created a physical being, there remained no hope of his freedom from disease; it was meaningless to think of him as originally spotless, but later fallen from grace. Vice like disease could not have been superimposed after the Creation, but must have been potential in every created being.[40]

Priestly concurred:

> With respect to the fall of Adam, all that we can learn from the Scriptures, interpreted literally, is, that the laborious cultivation of the earth, and the mortality of his race, were the consequences of it.[41]

In addition to Priestly and Rush, Jefferson also corresponded with a number of other prominent Unitarians, including Jared Sparks, minister, historian, and early president of Harvard College, Thomas Cooper, Benjamin Waterhouse, and President John Adams. Each of these figures had a personal theology that did not include belief in the divinity of Jesus, original sin, the Trinity, and other traditional beliefs of the Christian church.

Jefferson shared with Waterhouse the belief that Christianity had been corrupted early on by Saint Paul and Christian Platonists. He wrote to Cooper about the divinity of Jesus, to Adams about all kinds of religious issues, and to Sparks their shared beliefs in the moral sense being innate. Jefferson shared many beliefs with members of the Unitarian Church, many of whom were his close friends.

Unitarian Claims about Jefferson

Although Thomas Jefferson did not appear to number himself among the Unitarians, the Unitarians have claimed him as a member for generations. Since the mid-nineteenth century, the Unitarian Church repeatedly has made the claim that five Presidents of the United States were Unitarians—John Adams, John Quincey Adams, Millard Fillmore, William Howard Taft, and Thomas Jefferson. Garrison Keillor, on an episode of *The Prairie Home Companion*, pointed out that the Unitarians have "put more people on stamps and coins than just about any other denomination."[42] Presumably, Keillor had Jefferson and others in mind.

Unitarian-Universalist writer, Peg Duthie also wrote a recent article in the *UUWorld*, a Unitarian-Universalist magazine, entitled, "Was Thomas Jefferson Really One of Us?"[43] Duthie's conclusion is this:

> The consensus seems to be that he [Jefferson] had strong Unitarian sympathies but he did not formally belong to any Unitarian church.[44]

Duthie also points out that at a General Assembly of the Unitarian-Universalists in the 1990s, a group of African-Americans expressed outrage that the UU Church had planned to celebrate the two hundred fiftieth anniversary of Jefferson's birth. Indeed, by a vote of 75 to 51, the members of the UUA's Thomas Jefferson District voted to remove the name Thomas Jefferson from their organization.

George Chryssides, in his book, *The Elements of Unitarianism*, rightly suggests that the Unitarians' claim that Jefferson was one of them is exaggerated. Chryssides writes:

> Unitarians may have been prone to exaggerate the membership of their Hall of Fame, but equally there are historical figures who have been Unitarians, but who concealed their religious identity for fear of disapproval, sometimes preferring the more general designation "Christian." . . . Yet, whatever the nature of their links, it is undoubtedly true that Unitarians have produced an undue preponderance of men and women who have made important contributions to society. Indeed, the well-known writer Vance Packard said, "The Unitarian Church, tiny in total number, out ranks all denominations in the number of eminent Americans who have claimed it as their church."[45]

Despite these comments by Chryssides and Packard, the point remains that nowhere in the historical record did Thomas Jefferson suggest he was a member of the Unitarian Church. Although he had clear leanings and sympathies for the Unitarians, and he admired Priestly and other famous members of the Unitarian Church, we can end this chapter confidently by saying that Thomas Jefferson was not a Unitarian.

Conclusions

In this second chapter we have attempted several tasks. First, we gave an analysis of what it meant in the late eighteenth century to be called, or to call oneself a "Unitarian." In that analysis, we suggested an eighteenth-century Unitarian was one who denied the doctrine of the Trinity and the divinity of Jesus, while believing in the unity of God. Before that analysis, we gave a short history of anti-trinitarian ideas going back to Arius, and continuing through Michael Servetus and other Reformation thinkers like the Racovians in the sixteenth century who were also deniers of the doctrine of the Trinity. We then explored in this chapter the Unitarian golden age, the period in the late eighteenth and early nineteenth centuries when Thomas Jefferson was most attracted to Unitarian ideas.

In this period, Jefferson was most attracted to the theological point of view of Joseph Priestly, as well as several of Jefferson's Unitarian friends. Indeed, Jefferson goes far enough to say in a letter to Benjamin Waterhouse that at the time, 1825, he was a Unitarian.[46]

As we have seen in this chapter Priestly's influence on the theology of Thomas Jefferson was immense. More than any other figure, the works of Joseph Priestly that were read by Thomas Jefferson at the end of his life were a major factor in the President's religious beliefs. From Priestly, Jefferson inherited the idea of the unity of God, and the view that Christian doctrine had been corrupted by Greek philosophy and the role of the clergy in the early church. Jefferson also inherited from Priestly the Englishman's denial of beliefs in the Trinity, the divine nature of Jesus, the atonement, original sin, and the Virgin Birth, all ideas that Jefferson and Priestly saw as extra-biblical.

We have suggested that what Jefferson meant by that was that he was staunchly against Athanasius's formulation of the Trinity, and that he was just as skeptical, as Priestly and others were, with other traditional doctrines of the Christian church, views inconsistent with Unitarianism. Thus, the proper answer to the question raised at the beginning of this chapter is yes and no. Jefferson had a theology that mirrored the beliefs of the Unitarians, but he never joined their ranks.[47]

Notes

1. The version of the Nicene Creed we use in this chapter is John Behr, *The Nicene Faith: Formation of Christian Theology* (Crestwood, N.Y.: St. Vladimir's Seminary Press, 2004).

2. This text is known as the Codex Argenteus, and is owned by the University Library of Uppsala. The Codex is written in silver and gold letters on purple vellum. It is dated around 520, and most likely was produced in Ravenna. Of the 336 original leaves, only 188 remain. One leaf was discovered in 1970 in the Cathedral of Speyer in Germany.

   The manuscript was discovered in the middle of the sixteenth century in a Benedictine monastery of Werden, near Essen. Later it was owned by Emperor Rudolf II. In the last years of the Thirty Years War, the codex was subsequently deposited in the Library of Queen Christina in Stockholm. It was later sold to a Dutch scholar, Isaac Vossius, who sold it to Swedish Count, Magnus Gabriel de la Gardi. In 1669, Gardi gave the codex to the Uppsala Library. The most recent scholarship on the Codex Argenteus has been done by Lars Munkammar. His book, *Codex Argeneus: From Ravena to Uppsala*, was published in 1998.

3. William Ellery Channing, "Unitarian Christianity," a lecture delivered at the ordination of Jared Sparks, May 5, 1819, First Independent Church, Baltimore, Maryland.

4. Ibid.

5. Ibid.

6. Theodore, Parker, "A Discourse of the Transient and Permanent in Christianity" (Boston: B. H. Greene, 1842).

7. Ralph Waldo Emerson, *Nature* (New York: Penguin, 1982); *The American Scholar* (Princeton: Princeton University Press, 2003); *On Self Reliance* (New York: Library of America, 2005); Henry David Thoreau, *Walden* (New York: Houghton Mifflin, 2004).

8. Emanuel Swedenborg, *Heavenly Secrets: Arcana Coelestia* (Swedenborg Foundation, 1998); *The True Christian Religion* (Westchester, Pa: Swedenborg Foundation, 1947) For more on Swedenborg, see Erland J. Brock (ed.), *Swedenborg and His Influence* (Bryn Athyn, Pennsylvania: The Academy of the New Church, 1988). The most extensive treatment of Swedenborg remains R. L. Tafel, *Documents Concerning the Life and Character of Swedenborg*, 3 volumes (Westchester, Pa: Swedenborg Foundation, 1875–1877).

9. Immanuel Kant, *Traeume eines Geistersehers* (Konigsberg, 1760.) The most recent English edition is *Kant on Swedenborg: Dreams of a Spirit-Seer and Other Writings* (Westchester, Pa: Swedenborg Foundation, 2003).

10. Johann August Ernesti, *Principles of Biblical Interpretation*, translated by Charles H. Terrot, 2 volumes (Edinburgh: T. & T. Clark, 1832–1833).

11. B. F. Barrett wrote a life of Swedenborg, published in New York in 1842; Henry James's *The Secret of Swedenborg* (Boston, 1869) was the theologian's most extensive treatment of Swedenborg; Emerson's essay on Swedenborg, "Swedenborg: Or the

Mystic," was published in his *Representative Men* in 1850; and William Ellery Channing's view of Swedenborg is discussed in Julian Smith and William Wunsch, *The Gist of Swedenborg* (Philadelphia: Lippincott, 1920).

12. Jefferson to William Canby, September 18, 1813.

13. Jefferson to Benjamin Waterhouse, June 26, 1822.

14. Ibid.

15. Jefferson to Francis Adrian Van der Kemp on July 30, 1816.

16. Jefferson to Jared Sparks, November 4, 1820.

17. Jefferson to Thomas Cooper, November 2, 1822.

18. Ibid.

19. Ibid.

20. Jefferson to Benjamin Waterhouse, January 8, 1825.

21. Jefferson to J.P.P. Derieux, July 25, 1788.

22. Ibid.

23. Jefferson to James Smith, February 21, 1825.

24. Jefferson to John Adams, August 22, 1813.

25. Thomas Jefferson, Letter to William Short, October 31, 1819.

26. Thomas Jefferson, Letter to Timothy Pickering, February 27, 1821.

27. Eugene Sheridan, *Jefferson and Religion* (Charlottesville: Thomas Jefferson Foundation, 1998) 26.

28. Thomas Jefferson to Joseph Priestly, March 21, 1801.

29. Ibid.

30. Andrew Burstein, *Jefferson's Secrets: Death and Desire at Monticello* (New York: Basic Books, 2005) 241.

31. Ibid, 242.

32. Ibid.

33. Jefferson to Joseph Priestly, January 27, 1800.

34. Jefferson to Priestly, January 29, 1804.

35. Jefferson to Benjamin Rush, September 23, 1800.

36. Jefferson to Thomas Cooper, November 2, 1822.

37. Jefferson to John Adams, July 5, 1814.

38. Ibid.

39. Jefferson to John Adams, July 5, 1814.

40. Daniel J. Boorstin, *The Lost World of Thomas Jefferson* (Chicago: University of Chicago Press, 1993) 149.

41. Joseph Priestly, *Lectures on History and General Policy* (Philadelphia, 1803) Volume 1, 98.

42. Howard Dana, "Was Thomas Jefferson a Unitarian?" Sermon delivered March 7, 2004. The Unitarian Church of Harrisburg, Harrisburg, Pennsylvania.

43. Peg Duthie, "Was Thomas Jefferson Really One of Us?" *UUWorld* (Boston: Unitarian-Universalist Association, 2004). This text is from a sermon delivered at the First Unitarian-Universalist Church of Nashville, Tennessee.

44. Ibid.

45. George Chyrssides, *The Elements of Unitarianism* (Boston: Element, 1998) 82.

46. Jefferson to Benjamin Waterhouse, June 26, 1822.

47. For more on the issue of whether Thomas Jefferson was a Unitarian, see *What Kind of A Chrsitian Was Thomas Jefferson?* (Philadelphia: American Unitarian Assocation, 1947); also see, David E. Bumbaugh, *Unitarian Universalism: A Narrative History* (Chicago: Meadville Lombard Press, 2001); and Peg Duthie, "Was Thomas Jefferson Really One of Us?" (Boston: *UUWorld* 2002). All three works claim that Thomas Jefferson was a Unitarian, and give convincing evidence for that conclusion.

3 Was Thomas Jefferson a Deist?

*I have a view of the subject which ought to displease neither the
rational Christian nor Deists, and would reconcile many to a
character they have too hastily rejected.*

—Thomas Jefferson
   Letter to Benjamin Rush
   September 23, 1800

*Denominated a Deist, the reality of which I have never disputed,
being conscious that I am no Christian.*

—John Adams
   Letter to Thomas Jefferson
   December 25, 1813

*Some books against Deism fell into my hands . . . It happened that
they wrought an effect on me quite contrary what was intended by
them; for the arguments of the Deists, which were quotes to be refuted,
appeared to me stronger than the refutations. In short, I soon became
a Deist.*

—Benjamin Franklin
   Autobiography

Introduction

IN THIS CHAPTER, we take up the following tasks. First, we shall explore the origins and nature of the late eighteenth-century philosophical movement, Deism. Second, we will examine what influences contemporary Deists might have had on Thomas Jefferson. Third, we will examine several places in Jefferson's written works where the President mentions or discusses Deism and Deists. Finally, we will make some general conclusions about Jefferson's views on Deism. As we shall see, the proper answer to the question posed in the title of this chapter—like the answer posted in Chapter Two—is yes and no.

The most important conclusion to be made in this chapter is that Thomas Jefferson did not consider himself to be a Deist. Several pieces of evidence will be used in this chapter to arrive at that conclusion. Although Jefferson appears to have had a number of beliefs he shared with his Deist contemporaries, he did not, nevertheless, include himself among the ranks of Deism.

We will begin this chapter with a discussion on the origins and nature of the philosophical movement known as Deism. One of the most important conclusions about Deism, as we shall see, is that the movement did not arise in the eighteenth century when it was most popular.

The Origins and Nature of Deism

The origins and meaning of the term Deism are a matter of some great dispute. Some scholars suggest Deism began in the sixteenth century with the Socinians to contrast their opinion on God with atheism. More recently, the term has come to mean a movement of thought in the seventeenth and eighteenth centuries, mostly in England, France, and America, that attempted to replace revelation with the light of reason.

Other scholars suggest the origins of Deism to be found in the work of Edward Herbert of Cherbury (1583–1648), an English philosopher and an early modern explorer of several issues in epistemology. Herbert also wrote a great deal on the relationship of faith to reason. Most contemporary interest in Herbert, however, centers on his role as the founder of Deism.

Herbert believed there are five common notions in Deism. James M. Byrne sums them up this way:

1. There is a Sovereign God.

2. This Deity must be worshipped.

3. Piety is closely linked to virtue, to good living.

4. Wrongdoing must be expiated by repentance.

5. There is a reward or punishment after this life.[1]

Byrne continues his analysis:

Each of these Common Notions contains further refinements which defend and expand upon the general concept. For example, under the first and basic notion that there exists a Supreme Being, Herbert delineates eight qualities of God, among which are that God is cause of all that is good, and that God is the end of all things, and that God is eternal, just, and wise.[2]

Peter Byrne, in his book *Natural Religion and the Nature of Religion: The Legacy of Deism* suggests that the principal difference between Deism and traditional Theism is "a distinction between a supposed act of divine truths specially communicated by God in history and a real system of truths available to all by the use of unaided reason."[3] Byrne believes that Jefferson saw no need for revelation, dogmas, and rituals and other ideas in Christian revealed religion.

Russell Kirk provides a definition of Deism in his *The Roots of the American Order*. Kirk says:

> Deism was neither a Christian schism nor a systematic philosophy, but rather a way of looking at the human condition . . . The Deist professed belief in a single, Supreme Being, but rejected a large part of Christian doctrine . . . For the Deists, the Supreme Being indeed was the creator of the universe, but he did not interfere with the functioning of his creation.[4]

Kirk, Peter Byrne, and James Byrne all would agree that Deism is a belief in one God, who created the universe and then let it to run on its own.

The Latin phrase *deus absconditis* ("the God who went away") is often used by writers in France and England in the late eighteenth century to describe the Deist's version of theism. The term was first used by Pierre Bayle in the late seventeenth century, and continued well into Jefferson's day.

Additionally, the Deists rejected many of the traditional doctrines of Christianity, particularly the Trinity, the dual natures of Jesus, and miracles. When we use the word Deism in this chapter that is what we mean by the term. It is a definition embodied by Edward Herbert's five points, as well as most modern scholars of the Enlightenment.

Herbert's *De Veritate* ("On Truth"), written in 1624, laid down the principles that later Deists were to draw upon. Matthew Tindal (1653–

1733), called himself a "Christian Deist."[5] In his day, Tindal's *Christianity as Old as the Creation* was known as "the Deist's Bible."[6]

Later English Deism

Another of the earliest of English Deists was Charles Blount (1654–1693). His book, *Religio Laici* (Religion for the Laity) was published in 1683. It was based on a book by the same name by Edward Herbert published in 1645. Blount also published *Oracles of Reason*, which contains a chapter entitled, "A Summary Account of the Deist Religion"—the earliest known published statement of Deist beliefs. Blount rejected the Trinity and what he called "substitutionary Atonement." He also questioned the stories of Jesus' miracles, and he believed, as Jefferson did, that much of traditional Christianity had been invented by priests and other religious leaders.

John Locke (1632–1704), great English philosopher and political theorist, published a defense of Christianity he entitled, *The Reasonableness of Christianity* in 1695.[7] Locke suggests that although religion is not contrary to reason and Divine revelation, he claimed that religion must be understood in light of the tenets of reason. Thus, Locke, like the other Engish Deists, rejected many traditional Christian beliefs like the Trinity, the virgin birth, and the dual natures of Jesus. Locke believed if something cannot be provided through reason, then it ought not be assented to.

Locke was also an early proponent of religious toleration. In his *Letter Concerning Toleration*, a copy of which was in Jefferson's personal library at Monticello, the English philosopher make a number of arguments that are later to be found in Jefferson's *Notes on the State of Virginia*, as well as in Jefferson's writings of the founding documents of this country.

Speaking of religious toleration, Locke writes in *A Letter Concerning Toleration*:

> Nobody, therefore, in fine, neither single persons, not churches may, nor even commonwealths, have any just title to invade the civil rights and worldly goods of each other upon pretence of religion.[8]

Locke speaks not only of the religious toleration of one man for another, he also writes of the duties that magistrates have with reference to the rights pertaining to religious toleration. In the *Letter*, Locke suggests no magistrate should "prescribe by law nor compel by punishment"[9] any religious belief. Jefferson's copy of *Of Civil Government and Toleration* was well-marked and underscored. It is clear that the philosophy of John Locke was one of Thomas Jefferson's philosophical underpinnings.

Locke's *Reasonableness of Christianity* was followed a year later by John Toland's *Christianity Not Mysterious*.[10] Toland (1670–1722) was an Irish philosopher who was educated at Glasgow, Edinburgh, and Oxford. In his book, Toland suggests that what is mysterious and supernatural in Christianity must be discarded.

Toland suggests that any doctrine was "mysterious" or beyond human comprehension was not an essential part of the Christian faith. He argues that God would not expect human beings to believe anything that goes beyond human comprehension or that is contrary to reason. Toland's *Christianity Not Mysterious* was burned in Ireland and the Church of England eventually brought charges against Toland.

The opposition to English Deism was immediately intense. To defend the established Anglican Church a number of laws were passed in the latter half of the seventeenth century, suggesting that any attack on traditional Christianity could lead to punishments ranging from a fine to loss of public office or basic rights, like the right to own land. A second offence, these laws suggest, could lead to imprisonment.

Woolston believed that many of the events recorded in the Old and New Testaments should not be understood in a literal or historical sense, but rather should be interpreted allegorically. Among examples he gave were the Virgin Birth, the miracles of Jesus, and the Trinity. Woolston was imprisoned for "blasphemy," which was both a civil and a religious offense.

Indeed, this was the fate of Thomas Woolston (1670–1731), who lost his post at Cambridge for teaching against the miracles of Jesus. Woolston was fined and sentenced to a year in prison, where he died in 1731, unable to pay the fine imposed by the court. Woolston also argued for an allegorical interpretation of scripture, something else the authorities found unorthodox.[11]

Thomas Chubb (1679–1746), a self-taught English Deist, also regarded himself as a Christian Deist. Chubb was a champion for understanding religion in reasonable terms, while at the same time being skeptical of miracles, prophecy, revelation, and the efficacy of prayer. Chubb's principal works include: *The Supremacy of the Father Asserted* (1715); *A Discourse Concerning Reason* (1731); *The True Gospel of Jesus Christ Asserted* (1732); and *The True Gospel of Jesus Christ Vindicated* (1739).[12] Chubb (1679–1747) was a humble candle-maker and brilliant writer. In his book, *The True Gospel of Jesus Christ Asserted*, published in 1739, Chubb claimed he was a "Christian Deist," and he says that his books bring Deism to "ordinary people."

Thomas Morgan (1695–1743) was an ordained Presbyterian minister and later became a medical doctor. In his book, *The Moral Philosopher*, published in 1737, Morgan also identifies himself as a "Christian Deist." Like Jefferson, Morgan thought the truths of Christianity were all consistent with the truths of reason. In addition to the English Deists mentioned above, two other figures from the English Enlightenment are worthy of some mention for their influence on Thomas Jefferson. The first of these figures is Henry Saint John, the First Viscount of Bolingbroke (1678–1751). Bolingbroke was a political philosopher who made an immense impression on the philosophical ideas of Thomas Jefferson. Jefferson read Bolingbroke's *Works* with some approval, and he copied several passages from it in his *Commonplace Books*.[13]

The other English Enlightenment figure, besides Priestly and Bolingbroke, to have a direct influence on the religious ideas of Jefferson was Anthony Ashley Cooper, the Third Earl of Shaftesbury (1671–1713). Shaftesbury's *Characteristics of Men, Manners, Opinions, and Times,* is a three volume work published in 1711. Jefferson owned a copy of the *Characteristics*. Jefferson copied a number of passages from it in his *Commonplace Books*.[14] Jefferson's interest in Shaftesbury comes in two principal areas, the Englishman's views of religious toleration and his theory of ethics.

In his *Notes on the States of Virginia*, Jefferson outlines for the first time his view of religious toleration. Sanford suggests Jefferson's sources for the idea. "Jefferson was indebted to his wide reading, particularly from John Locke, Lord Shaftesbury, and John Milton, for many of these ideas on toleration."[15]

The other interest Jefferson has for Shaftesbury is his moral theory. The Englishman argues that the human ability to distinguish right from wrong is innate. He suggests that the ability to discern virtue in action is comparable to seeing beauty in art. Shaftesbury also sees that humans have a natural tendency toward benevolence, social interest, and commitment to the common good. This view of ethics was very attractive to Jefferson. It was at odds with the views of Hobbes that ethics derives from rational self-interest, something that Jefferson was staunchly against.

In a later section of this chapter, "Jefferson on Deism," we describe in more detail the influence that Bolingbroke and Shaftesbury had on Thomas Jefferson. It is enough now to say that Jefferson had a high regard for both of these English scholars, and he frequently quotes from them in his *Commonplace Books*.

Deism in France

The term "Deism" came into wide use in French toward the end of the seventeenth century. Pierre Bayle's *Dictionary* included an entry on Deism. Bayle refers to Deism as a term used to describe John Calvin's follower, Pierre Viret. Viret, Bayle tells us, describes a Deist as one who believes in a Creator God, but who rejected revelation and the divinity of Jesus.[16]

In France in the eighteenth century the word Deism was often used as being equivalent to Atheism. This accounts for the mention in chapter two that many of Jefferson's critics referred to the President as a "French infidel." A number of thinkers in France in the second half of the eighteenth century were thought to be both atheists and Deists. Chief among these thinkers were the Baron d' Holbach, Denis Diderot, Peter Viret, and Voltaire.

Peter Annet (1693–1769) was a French schoolmaster and prolific writer. His *Deism Fairly Stated*, was published in 1744. Annet suggests that "Deism ... is not other than the Religion essential to Man, the true, original religion of Reason and Nature." Annet thought this was the religion practiced by Socrates and others of old, and like Jefferson, Annet believed Christianity had been corrupted, chiefly by Saint Paul.

Denis Diderot whose *Encyclopedie* includes an entry on Deism. In that entry, Diderot suggests that Deists hold a materialist's understanding of psychology and ethics, and that the origins of their beliefs were Thomas Hobbes and David Hume, both of whom believed, as Jefferson did, that the human moral sense in innate. Jean-Jacques Rousseau also held this view. He called these instincts "moral sentiments," which he distinguishes from "acquired ideas."

Of the remaining French thinkers, the most influential was Voltaire (1694–1778). Voltaire paid close attention to the English Deists before him. Indeed, he refers to a number of them in his writings. Other French radicals of the day also followed the English Deists in believing that God created the universe, and then left it to run on its own. Voltaire and others advocated for a religious reform in France, not all that different from the one that already had taken place in England.

Voltaire was also attracted to the works of Newton and John Locke. He saw England as a useful model for a religious revolution in France. Voltaire distrusted democracy. In his view, only an enlightened monarch, advised by philosophers like himself, could bring about the necessary religious change. Jefferson knew the work of Voltaire. The Frenchman was influential in Jefferson's view of seeing certain stories in the Old Testament as "fables or allegories." Voltaire wanted a philosophy stripped of its religious roots.

Voltaire's chief opponent in France was Jean-Jacques Rousseau, who distrusted the aristocracy because he believed they were shunning traditional Christian values. Voltaire and Rousseau also argued over equality, which the former thought impossible, and the latter thought it to be the main force of a revolution to come.

Jefferson knew the work of Voltaire. Indeed, he rejected the Frenchman's explanation of how sea shells could be found at Monticello, well above sea level. Voltaire has written something about spontaneous shells appearing in a place near Tours. After reading Voltaire's report, Jefferson changed the text of *Notes on the State of Virginia* to reflect Voltaire's view of the shells. Eventually, Malone reports, Jefferson again changed his mind, adopting his original observations.[17]

Jefferson also suggests in Query VI of *Notes on the State of Virginia*, that Voltaire or Racine have the same place in French literature that

Homer had in Greece, Virgil in Latin, and Shakespeare and Milton have in English.[18]

Peter Gay, in commenting on Voltaire's religion tells the story of Voltaire inviting a friend to watch a sunrise together. On the top of a hill where they had gone, Voltaire knelt on the ground and began to pray, "I believe in you powerful God, I believe! As to my companions, his son, and madame his mother, that's a different story."[19]

In his *Philosophical Dictionary*, Voltaire defines a "Theist" the way we think of Deism, a believer in a minimal religion which reveres a Creator but omits most of the elements of traditional Christianity like the efficacy of prayer, miracles, Divine revelation, the incarnation, the divinity of Jesus, belief in the Trinity, and the damnation of souls to hell. This may well be what Voltaire meant when he said, "I believe in you powerful God." If this is so, then Jefferson's brand of religion may not be all that different from that of Voltaire, as we shall see in the next section of this chapter.

As time progressed in eighteenth-century France, the struggles over religion became sharpened. Writers like Diderot and d' Holbach went well beyond Voltaire's beliefs, extending this opposition to all Christian dogma, as well as belief in God, on whom they blamed all evil and suffering of the world.[20]

Although Jefferson shares a great deal about religion with both the English and French Deists, it is more likely that Jefferson and the French Deists were influenced by the English Deists than the other way around. In fact, in a letter written to John Adams on August 22, 1813, Jefferson explicitly says that he has been influenced by Joseph Priestly and English Deist, Conyers Middleton. About them, Jefferson writes, "I rest on them as a basis of my own faith."[21]

Conyers Middleton (1683–1750) in his later writings sought to bridge the gulf between sacred and profane. His *Inquiry into Miraculous Powers*, published in 1748, points out that miracles are common in primitive Christianity and in what he calls "heathen religion," in much the same way that Hume makes the same claim in his essay "Of Miracles."[22] The year before, 1747, Middleton published his *Introductory Discourse and the Free Inquiry*.[23] This work, as well, was "concerning the miraculous powers which are supposed to have subsisted in the church from its earliest ages." In this book, which was owned by Jefferson, Middleton establishes two propositions of capital importance. First, that church miracles must be accepted in the masses. And secondly, the authority of the early testimonials for miracles must be weighed against the claims of contemporary reason.[24] Before moving on to Jefferson's view of Deism, we can conclude that Deists in Jefferson's time held a belief system not all that different from Voltaire's. The Deists believed in a minimalist religion that accepts a Creator/Designer God, while withholding belief from many traditional Christian dogmas, such as the Trinity, the divinity of Jesus, miracles, original sin, Divine revelation, and the condemning of souls to hell.

It must be pointed out, however, that for Jefferson's contemporaries there was little difference between Atheist, Deist, and Infidel. All three were suspected as being enemies to Christianity, and against the well-being of society. As Jefferson says in one of his letters, "They [priests] wish me to be thought of as Atheist, Deist, or Devil."[25]

American Deism

Some of the earliest of American Deists were Revolutionary War heroes like Ethan Allen and Thomas Paine. Allen's *Reason the Only Oracle of Man* (1784) and Paine's *Age of Reason* (1794–1796) both launched savage attacks on orthodox Christianity. Both men also advocated Deism, a system of thought that dispensed with divine revelation, and ridiculed the divinity of Christ. Both Allen and Paine exalted human reason, and believed that religion is mostly about ethics.[26]

Although Deism never became popular among Americans, in the final two decades of the eighteenth century, it was the rage among American college students. At Princeton in 1782, only two students professed traditional Christianity. Bishop Merade wrote that the College of William and Mary had become a hotbed of French skepticism. Lyman Beecher, in commenting on the fact that only five students at Yale belonged to the college church, wrote, "That was the day of the infidelity of the Tom Paine school. Boys that dressed flax in the barn, as I used to, read him, and believed him."

Paine carefully outlines his view of Deism in the *Age of Reason*. It was there he writes:

The religion that approaches the nearest of all others to true Deism, in the moral and benign part thereof, is that of the Quakers.[27]

In another section of the *Age of Reason*, Paine says:

How different is Christianity to the pure and simple Deism! The true Deist has but one deity, and his religion consists in contemplating the power, wisdom, and benignity of the Deity in his works, and in endeavoring to imitate him in everything moral, scientifical, and mechanical.[28]

Paine's *Common Sense*, a monograph published anonymously in January, 1776, spread quickly among sophisticated colonists. Some estimate that 120,000 copies were distributed in the colonies. This work was one of the things that convinced George Washington and others to seek redress in political independence from Great Britain. Paine refused to call himself a "Christian," because the only "Christianity" he knew was the Trinitarian variety. Jefferson knew Paine well, and he had copies of his books in his library at Monticello.

Jefferson's association with Thomas Paine is described well in Joseph Ellis's *American Sphinx*:

By publically associating with Paine, Jefferson exposed himself to the full-broadside blasts of the Federalists press as an arch infidel, a "defiler of Christian virtue," and "a companion of the most vile, corrupt, obnoxious, sinner of the century.[29]

Ellis adds:

All Americans who took Christianity seriously now had to make a choice, said one editor, between "renouncing their savior, or their president."[30]

Benjamin Franklin (1706–1790) claimed to be a "thorough Deist" in his youth. He said that he "began to suspect that the doctrine might be true and useful." At the age of nineteen, Franklin adopted a Materialist philosophy, but later rejected it. Franklin was raised as a Calvinist. He attended a Presbyterian church in Philadelphia, but he stopped attending at the age of twenty. At that time, Franklin wrote a pamphlet entitled,

"Articles of Belief and Acts of Religion," and returned to his Deistic beliefs.

Historian Joyce Appleby points out that the fear of Deism was so popular in New England in Jefferson's day that by 1808 the Connecticut legislature passed a law making adherence to Deism a felony. She adds, "Only in retrospect does the issue of religious orthodoxy seem exaggerated."[31]

Opposition to Deism

In the English speaking world the most important opponent to Deism was Joseph Butler (1692–1752). Butler was Oxford educated and eventually became bishop of Bristol, Dean of St. Paul's, and the bishop of Durham in 1750. Butler's principal works include: *Fifteen Sermons* (1726) and *The Analogy of Religion and Dissertation Upon The Nature of Virtue*, published in 1736.

In these three works, Butler defended traditional Christianity against the Deists. Butler utilizes an analogy from Origen as the basis of his critique of Deism. Butler quotes Origen:

> Those who believe the Author of Nature to also be the Author of Scripture must expect to find in scripture the same sorts of difficulties that they find in Nature.[32]

A Deist might complain that scripture says that God visits inequities of the fathers upon their children of the third and fourth generation. How could that be fair? Butler replies by saying that nature does the same thing. A pregnant woman on crack gives birth to a daughter with a dependency. The daughter eventually gives birth to a daughter who also grows up to be dependent on crack.

Thus, Butler argues that nature shows the biblical dictum of inequities passed on to the third and fourth generations. But Butler suggests that Christianity adds grace to the equation. God may break the cycle of nature and sets things right. Butler also argues that the human conscience is strong support for the Christian claim to natural law and an innate view of the good, something not held by all the English Deists.

Another doubt that Butler raises about the Deists' view of Christianity says that if God is Love, then why is He so ruthless in the Old Testament, where He slays the first-born of Egypt, or He tells Israelites to kill everyone in the city of Jericho. Butler replies this way:

> Nature shows us entire towns destroyed by earthquakes or volca-
> noes, or plague. Worse, every human being eventually dies. Why
> is it consistent with the goodness of God to decide that everyone
> in Pompeii is to die now, and cause a volcano to kill them, but not
> consistent with the goodness of God to decide that everyone in
> Jericho is to die now, and order Joshua to kill them?[33]

Again, Butler uses the analogy of nature, and argues that the questions the Deists raise about the goodness of God may also be raised about nature itself. And that the goodness of nature is at the heart of the metaphysics of the Deists. Butler's books had a tremendous influence on David Hume, the eighteenth-century philosophical skeptic who did not admire most Christian apologists. Hume admired Butler, and had intended to dedicate one of his principal works to Butler.

In the *Analogy*, Butler also suggests analogies in nature to the death and resurrection of Christ. He uses the example of a caterpillar turning into a butterfly as a way of showing that what happens in the gospels also occurs in the natural world as well.

Before Butler and his *Analogy* another English philosopher, Henry Dodwell, also had a number of criticisms of Deism in his book, *Christianity Not Founded on Argument*, published in 1742. Dodwell (d. 1784) was engaged with Conyers Middleton over the issue of miracles, and defended traditional Christianity against the Deists.

Dodwell attempted to demonstrate the Deist's error constructing a basis for Christianity by arguing that the truth of religion is to be found in the nature of religious experience. He called for support of the traditional Christian miracles by way of religious experience. Dodwell also supported Tertullian's dictum "Credo quia absurdum," I believe because it is absurd.

David Hume's "Essay on Miracles," written in 1748, and his *Natural History of Religion* (1757) also were seen as simultaneously criticizing revealed religion, as well as the metaphysics of the Deists. At any rate, by the close of the eighteenth century Deism pretty much was dead.

Jefferson on Deism

Thomas Jefferson mentions Deism or Deists in a number of his letters. These mentions of the philosophical movement give us some sense of what he thought about Deism. In a letter to Benjamin Rush on September 23, 1800, Jefferson says:

> I promised you a letter on Christianity, which I have not forgotten. On the contrary, it is because I have reflected on it, that I find much more time necessary for it than I can at present dispose of. I have a view of the subject which ought to displease neither the rational Christian nor Deist, and would reconcile many to a character they have too hastily rejected.[34]

Jefferson seems to imply here that his view of religion is compatible with beliefs of both traditional Christianity and the Deists. In another letter at the end of his life, Jefferson suggests that the ancient Jews were believers in Deism. Jefferson comments "I should then take a view of the Deism and ethics of the Jews, and show in what a degraded state they were, and the necessity they presented of a reformation."[35]

This notion of Jefferson's that the ancient Jews were Deists is to be found in another letter to Benjamin Rush from April 21, 1803, where Jefferson writes:

> The Jews, their system was Deism; that is, the belief of one only God. But their ideas of him and of his attributes were degrading and injurious.[36]

Later in the same letter, Jefferson repeats the claim; when speaking of Jesus he says, "He corrected the Deism of the Jews, confirming them in their belief of one only God, And giving them juster notions of his attributes and government."[37] In another letter to John Adams from April 11, 1823, Jefferson discusses the "disciples of . . . Diderot and D'Holbach . . ." and a view of cosmology suggesting that the universe has always existed and thus was uncreated.[38] Later in the same letter, Jefferson argues against this view, and suggesting in its stead "that when we take a view of the Universe, in its parts, particular or general, it is impossible for human mind not to perceive and feel a conviction of design . . ."[39] Jefferson seems to be an advocate of the teleological argument for God's existence popular in the thinking of William Paley and others in his day. Paley (1743–1805), British philosopher and theologian, was the author of several books, including *Evidences of Christianity* (1794) and *Natural Theology* (1802),[40] published shortly before Paley's death. Jefferson owned a copy of this latter text. It was part of his personal library at Monticello.[41]

In another letter to John Adams on April 8, 1816, Jefferson confirms his belief in a Creator-Designer God:

> I say, for the human mind not to believe, that there is in all this, design, cause and effect, up to an ultimate cause, a Fabricator of all things from matter and motion.[42]

In Jefferson's study notes, he copied approvingly the works of Henry St. John Bolingbroke. Lord Bolingbroke (1672–1751), wrote a number of political and philosophical tracts. His philosophical works show him to have been a Deist. He believed in God, as Jefferson did, but rejected revelation. Goldsmith in his *Life of Lord Bolingbroke* suggests that on his death bed Lord Bolingbroke gave orders that "none of the clergy should be permitted to trouble him in his last moments."[43]

Henry Saint John (1672–1751), the Viscount of Bolingbroke, was a prominent politician of the day who served as Secretary of State and Secretary of War in various administrations of the British Empire. Bolingbroke studied philosophy, became a Deist, and was a friend of Voltaire's. Bolingbroke's belief in the existence of God was based on a teleological argument. He said, "When we contemplate the works of God . . . they give us a clear and determined idea of the wisdom and power of God, which we call infinite."

From Bolingbroke, Jefferson copied, "Modern discoveries in astronomy have presented the works of God to us in a more noble scene."[44] Jefferson also copied a long passage from French deist Claude Helviticus (1715–1771) about how "the order and movement" of the universe is evidence for "an unknown force and cause of that which is."[45]

Jefferson also copied in his notes a number of passages from Bolingbroke, where the Englishman had objected to seeing the Divine in anthropomorphic ways. Bolingbroke was also the source of Jefferson's belief that the ancient Jews were Deists. Bolingbroke also believed, as Jefferson later did, that this Deism of the Jews needed reform that was supplied by Jesus Christ. Jefferson also gleaned from Bolingbroke a number of Old Testament passages that show the Hebrew Bible's lack of scientific understanding, particularly in cosmology.

All this evidence suggests that Jefferson agrees with the various Deists on a number of different issues, including belief in a Creator-Designer God; a rejection of many traditional Christian beliefs such as revelation, the Trinity, and the divinity of Jesus. Jefferson seems to have picked and chosen from the beliefs of various Deists, Unitarians, and Atheists. He did not, for example, adopt Priestly's belief in resurrection of the body, but instead followed the beliefs of Voltaire and Matthew Tindal, who rejected the biblical accounts of the resurrection as "allegories, fables, and unhistoric extravagant stories."[46]

Other evidence that Jefferson shares the Deist's belief in a Creator-Designer God are the many other terms he uses to describe God, when he does not use that term. Robert M. Healy in his *Jefferson on Religion in Public Education*, indicated that Jefferson uses twenty-six different terms for God.[47] Included in these are: "Preserver and Regulator," "Creator of it all," "Fabricator," "Intelligent and Powerful Agent," "Supreme Ruler," "Nature's God," and "Common Father." All of these terms regularly were used by various of the Deist thinkers. Bolingbroke regularly employed "Nature's God," as does the *Declaration*. Voltaire uses "Nature's God," and the "Creator of All," in his poem, "Natural Law." Alexander Pope refers to God as the "Ruling Mind" in his "Essay on Man." Jefferson is in agreement, then, with these Enlightenment thinkers who prefer at times to avoid using the word "God," and often chose instead terms that both French and English Deists used to describe the deity.

Accusations of Jefferson as a Deist

Beginning very early on in Jefferson's public life, he was accused of being a Deist. Prior to the election of 1800, William Linn and others used the term to describe Jefferson's religious beliefs.

Joyce Appleby speaks of the Reverend Linn's accusation that Jefferson was a Deist:

> Citing passages from Jefferson's *Notes*, the Reverend William Linn warned that anyone who avowed such things [Deism] would destroy religion, introduce immorality, all loosen all the bonds of society. "The voice of the nation is calling a Deist to the

first office must be construed into no less than a rebellion against God.[48]

The congregational preachers' belief that Jefferson was a Deist led them in 1808 to convince the Connecticut state legislators to make the practice of Deism a felony in the state. Timothy Dwight, the president of Yale describes the 1800 election as a choice between "God and a religious president or Jefferson and no God."[49] Thus, Jefferson was not only accused of Deism, he was also accused in his own time of immorality and atheism.

The accusation that Jefferson was a "French Infidel" was also an attempt to show that Jefferson is to be identified with French Deists or Atheists. Jefferson speaks specifically about these accusations in a letter to Mrs. Harrison Smith from August 6, 1816. In this letter, Jefferson writes about the various labels that had been assigned to him by his contemporaries:

> They wish me to be thought atheist, deist, or devil, who could advocate freedom from their religious dictations.[50]

In addition to Jefferson's contemporaries who frequently saw him as a Deist, many Jefferson scholars over the ages have seen him that way. Among late twentieth century to the present researchers, Dumas Malone's comment that Jefferson was accused of Atheism is a common one. Malone remarked, "It was not only made in the public press, it has hurled from pulpits in various places, most of all probably Connecticut. Actually, he was a Deist."[51] Malone is in good company. The claim that Jefferson was a Deist has been repeated by countless other modern scholars. Edwin Gaustad and Joseph Ellis, for examples, have both made the claim about Jefferson.[52] Edward Mahoney-Walter, in an article for the New York *Herald* suggests, "Jefferson and other founders were Deists, believing in a Universal God and a scientific universe."[53] Charles Sanford, writing in his *The Religious Life of Thomas Jefferson* remarks, "In private, deists like Jefferson and Paine had some reservations about the Old Testament and did not hesitate to correct the biblical account of creation ... "[54]

Constance Barlett Schulz, writing in her Ph.D. dissertation for the University of Cincinnati in 1973 also made the claim that Jefferson was a Deist.[55] Indeed, this charge that Jefferson was a Deist is the most prevalent point of view of Jefferson's religion in contemporary scholarship on the former president.

Contemporary scholar, Andrew Burnstein also makes the claim that Jefferson was a Deist. Burnstein writes:

> Thomas Jefferson was not what we would call an atheist, but a Deist, believing in a Creator who had set the laws of nature in motion but who did not interfere in human affairs.[56]

This observation of Burnstein's is not only held by many contemporary scholars, it was also, as we have shown, a common belief in Jefferson's day. But nowhere in the voluminous corpus of Jefferson's writings does our third president explicitly say, "I am a Deist."

Conclusions

Several conclusions arise from our discussion of Jefferson's supposed Deism in this chapter. First, like the chapters on atheism and the Unitarians, when Jefferson speaks of the Deists, he always does it in the third person. When Jefferson uses the term "Deism" it is usually talked about in a pejorative way. Indeed, most often he refers to Deists, along with atheists, devils, and infidels, often when he is speaking about his clergy critics in his day.

A second important conclusion in this chapter is that Jefferson was quite sympathetic to many of the beliefs of some of his Deistic contemporaries. Jefferson quoted liberally from Bolingbroke, Shaftesbury, and other Deists in his written works. Like many of these Deistic thinkers, Jefferson frequently avoids using the word "God," in favor of a number of other expressions like "Fabricator" and "Nature's God."

A third conclusion: Jefferson explicitly says in one of his letters that his religious views have been modeled after those of the Unitarian Priestly and the Deist Conyers Middleton. From Priestly, Jefferson gleaned his belief in one God, and the rejection of a whole host of traditional Christian religious propositions. From the Deist, Middleton, Jefferson borrowed the Englishman's idea that the story of the fall of man was a "fable, or allegory."[57]

A fourth and final conclusion is the realization that although Jefferson agrees with a number of Deists about a range of metaphysical questions, nowhere in Jefferson's entire corpus does the President say, "I am a Deist." As we saw in chapter two, Jefferson did say on occasion that he was a Unitarian, but he did not say a corresponding thing about Deism. What Jefferson did say about Deism is that when either the Deists or the traditional Christian discovers his religious beliefs, neither would be at odds with his beliefs. Thus, I think we can conclude that Jefferson was sympathetic to the beliefs of many of the Deist, particularly the English Deists, but he did not number himself among their ranks.

Notes

1. James Byrne, *Religion and the Enlightenment* (Louisville: Westminster John Knox, 1996) 104. For more on the history and contemporary perspectives on Deism, see James Barr, "Biblical Faith and Natural Theology," *The Grifford Lecture: The University of Edinburgh* (Oxford: Oxford University Press, 1959); Peter Gay, *Deism: An Anthology* (New York: Krieger, 1968); Kerry Walters, *The American Deists: Voices of Reason and Dissent* (Univerity of Kansas Press, 1992); and Samuel Chandler and James Foster, *History of British Deism* (London: Routledge, 1994).

2. Ibid.

3. Peter Byrne, *Natural Religion and the Nature of Religion: The Legacy of Deism* (London: Routledge, 1989) 17.

4. Russell Kirk, *The Roots of American Order* (Wilmington, Delaware: ISI Books, 2003).

5. James Byrne, 109.

6. Ibid.

7. John Locke, *The Reasonableness of Christianity* (Oxford: Oxford University Press, 2000).

8. John Locke, "A Letter Concerning Toleration," in *On Civil Government and Toleration* (London: Cassell's National Library, 1898) 157.

9. Ibid., 162.

10. John Toland, *Christianity Not Mysterious* (London: Thoemmes Continuum, 1999).

11. James Byrne, 109.

12. Thomas Chubb, *The Supremacy of the Father Asserted* (London, 1715.); *A Discourse Concerning Reason* (London, 1731); and *The True Gospel of Jesus Christ Vindicated* (London, 1739).

13. Thomas Jefferson, *Commonplace Books*, edited by Gilbert Chinard (Baltimore: Johns Hopkins University Press, 1926.)

14. Ibid.

15. Sanford, 24.

16. James Byne, 103.

17. Dumas Malone, *Jefferson and the Rights of Man*, Volume II (Boston: Little Brown and Company, 1951) 111–12 and 125–26.

18. Thomas Jefferson, "Notes on the State of Virginia," in *Works* (New York: The Library of America, 1984) 190.

19. Sanford, 84.

20. James Byrne, 134–43.

21. Jefferson to John Adams, August 22, 1813.

22. David Hume, "Of Miracles," Section X of *An Enquiry Concerning Human Understanding* (Oxford: Oxford University Press, 1975).

23. Conyers Middleton, *Introductory Discourse and the Free Inquiry* (London, 1747).

24. Ibid.

25. Jefferson to John Adams, April 11, 1823.

26. Ethan Allen, *Reason the Only Oracle of Man* (New York: Burt Franklin, 1972); Thomas Paine, *The Age of Reason* (New York: Carol, 1976).

27. Paine, 17.

28. Ibid., 22.

29. Joseph Ellis, *American Sphinx* (New York: Vintage, 1996) 257.

30. Ibid.

31. Joyce Appleby, *Thomas Jefferson* (New York: Henry Holt, 2003) 61.

32. James Byrne, 114.

33. Ibid., 115.

34. Jefferson to Benjamin Rush, September 23, 1800.

35. Jefferson to Samuel Kercheval, January 19, 1810.

36. Jefferson to Benjamin Rush, April 21, 1803.

37. Ibid.

38. Jefferson to Thomas Law, June 13, 1814.

39. Ibid.

40. Hannah More, *Works* Volume IX, 323.

41. Douglas Wilson, *Jefferson's Books* (Charlottsville, VA: Monticello Foundation).

42. Jefferson to John Adams, April 8, 1816.

43. Ian McCallum, "New Jerusalem: Prophecy, Dissent, and Radical Culture in England, 1786–1830," in Knud Haakonssen, *Enlightenment and Religion* (Cambridge: Cambridge University Press, 1996) 333.

44. Eugene Sheridan, *Jefferson and Religion* (Charlottsville: Thomas Jefferson Foundation, 1998) 16.

45. Ibid.

46. James Byrne, 95.

47. Robert M. Healy, *Jefferson on Religion in Public Education*, quoted in Sanford, 87.

48. Joyce Appleby, *Thomas Jefferson* (New York: Henry Holt, 2003) 60.

49. Ibid., 61.

50. Jefferson to Mrs. Harrison Smith, August 6, 1816.

51. Malone, Volume V, 190.

52. Joseph Ellis, *American Sphinx* (New York: Vintage Books, 1996) 256.; Edwin Gaustad, *Faith of the Founders: Religion and the New Nation* (Dallas: Baylor University Press, 2004) 156.

53. Edward Mahoney-Walter, "Jefferson's Religion," *New York Herald*, February 25, 1947.

54. Sanford, 85.

55. Constance Barlett Schultz, "The Radical Religious Ideas of Thomas Jefferson and John Adams: A Comparison," Ph.D. dissertation, University of Cincinnati, 1973.

56. Andrew Burnstein, *Jefferson's Secrets* (New York: Basic Books, 2005) 240.

57. Sanford, 62.

Was Thomas Jefferson a Christian?

But the greatest of all the reformers of the depraved religion of his country was Jesus of Nazareth.

—Thomas Jefferson

And the day will come when the mystical generations of Jesus, by the supreme being as his father in the womb of a virgin will be classed with the fable of the generation of Minerva in the brain of Jupiter. But may we hope that the dawn of reason and freedom of thought in these United States will do away with the artificial scaffolding, and restore to us the primitive and genuine doctrines of this most venerated reformer of human errors.

—Thomas Jefferson
  Letter to John Adams, April 11, 1823

If Jefferson were ever drawn into an attack on any Church, it was not because it was a religious organization but because it has assumed a political character, or because it limited, in one way or another, the freedom of the mind, on which he never ceased to believe the progress of the human species toward happiness depends.

—Dumas Malone
  Jefferson and the Rights of Man

Introduction

IN THIS FOURTH chapter, we will explore the question of whether Thomas Jefferson thought of himself as a Christian, and, as well, whether it is best to understand Thomas Jefferson's religious views as being consistent with traditional Christian doctrine. We will begin the chapter with a number of observations about Jefferson's early religious life, concentrating on his schooling before he entered William and Mary.

We will continue in this chapter discussing the view that Jefferson had some kind of religious awakening in his early time at William and Mary. In a third section of this chapter, we explore a number of comments that Jefferson made about Christianity in general, as well as Jesus Christ in particular.

At the close of this chapter, we make some general conclusions about an answer to the question posed in the title of this chapter. The most important of these conclusions is that Jefferson was a Christian in his early life, but did not consider himself a member of the Christian church in most of his adult life.

At times in his later life, Jefferson refers to himself as a follower of Christ, but these observations mostly were made in reference to Jesus' moral teachings. If Jefferson considered himself a Christian, it was because of these moral teachings, and not because of assent to more orthodox Christian dogma like belief in the Trinity or the dual natures of Jesus.

Jefferson's Early Religious Life

The earliest evidence we have of Thomas Jefferson's religious life comes from Henry Stephens Randall's nineteenth-century account of the life of Jefferson. Randall's three volume *The Life of Thomas Jefferson*, published in 1858, provides a wealth of information about Jefferson's early religious life.

Randall points out that Jefferson was baptized by an official of the Anglican Church. Randall makes a number of references to the Jefferson family Bible where the names and dates of baptisms, marriages, and deaths of family members were recorded. All these events also occurred in the Anglican faith.

In his early years, Thomas Jefferson was educated at home by family tutors. When Jefferson was two years old, Col. William Randolph, a close friend of Peter Jefferson, died. In Randolph's will, he requested that Peter Jefferson take over the education of his son, Thomas Mann Randolph. As Peter Jefferson's account books confirm, he hired a John Staples to educate the young Randolph.

John Staples remained in the employ of Peter Jefferson from 1750–1752. Thus, Thomas Jefferson was first educated, with Thomas Mann

Randolph as his classmate, and Mr. Staples as his teacher. In Jefferson's autobiography, he refers to these two years as "the English School."[1]

Jefferson was five years old when he began studying under John Staples at Tuckahoe. In 1752, the Jeffersons returned to Shadwell, and almost immediately Thomas was sent to Northam in Saint James Parish, Virginia, where he studies with the Reverend William Douglas. Thomas Jefferson was nine years old. The Rev. Douglas was a minister of the Scottish Presbyterian Church. He taught the young Jefferson Greek, Latin, and the basis for a gentleman's education. Jefferson, in his autobiography, refers to this period as "the Latin School."[2] James Madison was also a student of Douglas. Madison wrote of Douglas, "I had learned French from my Scotch tutor, reading it with him, as we did Greek and Latin. That is, as a dead language, and this too pronounced with his Scotch accent."[3]

Jefferson took to the classical languages, and used them regularly in the rest of his life. In his autobiography, Jefferson reveals he liked the Latin and Greek, but cared little for the Rev. Douglas, nor for his abilities.

In 1757, when Jefferson was fourteen, Peter Jefferson, his father, died at the age of forty-nine. A short time later, Jefferson became enrolled at the school of the Reverend James Maury, an Anglican priest. In his autobiography, Jefferson refers to Maury as a "correct classical scholar."[4] Jefferson was tutored by the Rev. Maury for two years. The subjects at the Maury School included: Latin, Greek, Classical Literature, Mathematics, French, and other subjects as well.

No description of the Rev. Maury exists in Jefferson's papers. In the memoir of the Rev. Jonathan Boucher, however, we find this:

> Rev. Mr. Maury, a native of Virginia, educated at William and Mary College, a singularly ingenuous and worthy man; who, with his numerous family, live in Albermarle County . . . Mr. Maury was of French parents; begotten, as he used to tell, in France, born at sea, reared in England, and educated in America.[5]

The Rev. Maury on July 17, 1862, wrote a letter to Robert Jackson, outlining his view of education. The letter was written on one hundred half sheets of paper, and is now called, the *Reverend Maury's Dissertation on Education*. In it, the Rev. Maury puts forth his view of the education of "Virginia Gentlemen born to an affluent Fortune," as well as others who may seek "a lucrative Business." The Rev. Maury's curriculum included "parts of literature," "a smattering of geography and history," "knowledge of laws, Constitution, and Religion of his country," and the study of "ancient languages."[6]

Jefferson admired Maury as a classical scholar, but did not admire him for his narrow views. He denounced anyone who did not belong to the Church of England, and eventually the Rev. Maury took Britain's side in the battle with the American colonies.

In 1760, at the age of seventeen, Jefferson began to feel he had learned all he could from the Rev. Maury. He wrote a letter to his guardian, John Harvie, and asked if he could attend the College of William and Mary in Williamsburg, the capital of the colony. In the Harvie letter, which is the earliest of Jefferson's extant letters, the young Jefferson argues that studying in Williamsburg would be cheaper than continuing with the Rev. Maury. Harvie conceded, and Jefferson made his way, along with his slave Jupiter, to William and Mary in March of 1760.

The letter to Harvie was written on January 14, 1760, from Shadwell. Jefferson writes:

> Sir:
>
> I was at Col. Peter Randolph's about a fortnight ago, and my Schooling falling into Discourse, he said he thought it would be to my advantage to go to college, and was desirous I should go, as indeed I am myself for several reasons. In the first place, as long as I stay on the Mountain the loss of one fourth of my time is inevitable, by Company's coming here and detaining me from School. And likewise, my Absence will be in a great measure put a stop to so much company, and by that Means lessen the expenses of the Estate in House-keeping. And on the other hand, by going to the College I shall get a more universal Acquaintance, which may hereafter be serviceable to me; and I suppose I can pursue my Studies in the Greek and Latin as well there as here, and likewise learn something of the Mathematics. I shall be glad of your opinion.
>
> Thomas Jefferson[7]

At William and Mary, Jefferson was taught by William Small, a Scot who had been educated at the University of Aberdeen. Small had become professor of philosophy at William and Mary in 1758. Soon after Jefferson's arrival in 1760, Small also assumed the duties of teaching moral philosophy, when the chair was left vacant by the departure of Jacob Rowe.

The best sources of Jefferson's education in this Williamsburg period are his *Commonplace Books*. Among Jefferson's reading at William and Mary were Horace, Aristotle, Tacitus, Publius, Cicero, Alexander Pope's translation of the *Iliad,* and Milton. Jefferson also read in this period the works of a number of French and English Enlightenment thinkers.

Jefferson says that Aristotle's *Politics* gave to the colonists "ideas of the value of personal liberty." He called Tacitus "the strongest writer in the world." Cicero gave the colonists their most "inspiring philosophy, the laws of nature."

Of the English thinkers, three stood out for Jefferson: Locke, Francis Bacon, and Isaac Newton. Of them, Jefferson later wrote, "Bacon, Locke, and Newton, the three greatest men who had ever lived, without exceptions." From Locke's *Second Treatise on Government* Jefferson copied lines like:

> Men being, as has been said, by nature and free, equal and independent, no one can be put out of this estate and subjected to the political power of another without his own consent.[8]

Jefferson adds:

> He, most happily for me, became soon attached to me & made me his daily companion when not engaged in the school; and from his conversation I got my first views of the expansion of science & of the system of things in which we are placed.[9]

William Small (1734–1775) was indeed a remarkable man. He was a graduate of Marischal College of the University of Aberdeen, and taught at William and Mary for six years from 1758 to 1764. Small left a great impression on the college's curriculum and the memories of his students.

Later in life, Dr. Small returned to Britain. He practiced medicine in Birmingham, and he became the center of a celebrated group called the Lunar Society. When Small died in 1775 at the age of forty-one, many were devastated by his death. His friend, Erasmus Darwin (Charles Darwin's grandfather) wrote this about William Small:

> His strength of reasoning, quickness of invention, learning in the discoveries of other men, and integrity of heart (which is worth them all) has no equal.[10]

Among the books Jefferson studied with William Small, books that were in his personal library at Monticello, were Euclid's *Elements* in the eighteenth-century Keill edition; William Emerson's *Doctrines of Fluxions*, and two of Isaac Newton's works, the *Principia* and the *Opticks*. It is also likely that Jefferson studied philosophy with William Small. Books by Hobbes, Locke, David Hume, and others were among the books in his personal library.

William Small introduced Jefferson to the writings of Newton, John Locke, and Francis Bacon, as well as early thinkers in the English Enlightenment. Jefferson thrived under the tutelage of Dr. Small. Jefferson later wrote of Small, "It was my great fortune, and what probably fixed the destinies of my life, that Dr. William Small of Scotland was then professor of mathematics, a man profound in most of the usual branches of science, with a happy talent of communication, correct and gentlemanly manners and an enlarged and liberal mind."[11]

Jefferson graduated from William and Mary in 1762. He went on to read law with the celebrated George Wythe, who later became the first professor of law at the college in 1779. Later Jefferson refers to Wythe as "my earliest and best friend. To him I am indebted for first impressions which have made the most salutary influence on the course of my life."

Through Small and Wythe, Jefferson met Governor Francis Fauquier. Jefferson frequently dined with these three older men at the Governor's Palace in Williamsburg. Jefferson said that the music concerts at the Palace were his "favorite passion of the soul." Indeed, Jefferson took part in these Palace musicales by playing the cello or piano.

Dumas Malone sums up Jefferson's years at William and Mary when he says

> Jefferson's student days in Williamsburg are the story of the . . . first flowering of an extraordinary mind.[12]

At William and Mary Jefferson became familiar with some of the best minds of his day, who also familiarized him with many of the great Enlightenment thinkers of his day. It was at William and Mary that Jefferson had his first encounters with the life of the mind, a vibrant life that would continue until his death.

Jefferson's Religious Crisis at William and Mary

Many of Jefferson's major biographers agree that our third president had some sort of religious crisis at William and Mary. Charles Sanford describes this crisis this way:

> When Jefferson went away from home to college at William and Mary, according to most of his biographers he was challenged by stimulating teachers and the deistic writers of the Enlightenment, lost the pious faith of his Anglican upbringing, and, after a period of doubt and crisis, developed a new rational religion.[13]

Sanford goes on to quote a letter written by Jefferson to Thomas Cooper that Gilbert Chinard cites as evidence that Jefferson had lost his faith in this period. In the letter, Jefferson recalls his "bold pursuit of knowledge," and his eagerness to fight "every authority which stood in the way of truth and reason."[14] This hardly seems evidence of a religious crisis. Nevertheless, Dumas Malone, Henry W. Foote, Henry Stephens Randall, James Truslow Adams, and Henry Lodge, all make the same claim about Jefferson's religious crisis in his college years.[15]

Others have argued that Jefferson's letter to his nephew, Peter Carr, written from Paris on August 10, 1787, about the boy's education, is further evidence that Jefferson may have gone through a religious crisis like his nephew might be experiencing as well. Jefferson instructs Carr about religion to "divest himself of all bias in favor of novelty and singularity of opinion."[16] Later in the same letter, Jefferson advises:

> Fix reason firmly in her seat, and call to her tribunal every fact, every opinion. Question with boldness even the existence of a God; because if there be one, he must approve of the homage of reason, than that of a blindfolded fear.[17]

Again, in the same letter, Jefferson advises Peter Carr, "Do not be frightened from this inquiry by any fear of its consequences."[18] The application of reason, Jefferson argues, sometimes results in a stronger religious view than faith and revelation do.

One crisis that Jefferson does admit to in his college days was his temptation to fall into the company of the wrong people—those who spend more time fox hunting or in the taverns than they did with their studies. He warned his grandson of these temptations when he went away to college.

Some suggest that Jefferson must have gone through a religious crisis when he arrived at William and Mary, for in Jefferson's advice to his nephew, he warns him that it is the sort of thing that happens when a boy first leaves home. The fact that Jefferson may have experienced a crisis in faith, as many college students do, is not an unusual state of affairs. In some ways, if it occurred it makes Jefferson look more like the rest of us. It makes Jefferson seem more human, and perhaps it explains some of the facts of his early intellectual life. But we must conclude with Charles Sanford on this matter, when he writes:

> Unfortunately, it does not adequately explain all the facts, and the evidence for such a crisis is scanty and weak.[19]

Indeed, among Jefferson scholars there are some who believe that Jefferson did not go through a religious crisis at William and Mary. In addition to Charles Sanford, Stuart Brown, another Jefferson scholar of note, believes that Jefferson did not go through a violent, emotional religious experience, where he lost his faith. The available evidence, as well, certainly does not suggest Jefferson had a religious crisis at William and Mary. Jefferson clearly learned about the Enlightenment in his years in Williamsburg, he became aware of the thinking of various Enlightenment thinkers, Deists, Theists, Atheists, and Unitarians in his college and law school days. We know he copied passages from many of these Enlightenment thinkers into his *Commonplace Books*.[20] But nowhere in the evidence does Jefferson make the claim that he is a member of one of these groups.

Whether or not Jefferson experienced a religious awakening at Williamsburg is not clear. Randall reports, however, that in those years our third president on a number of occasions refused to be a godfather at the baptisms of the children of friends, because he could not assent to the baptismal creed of the day that included belief in the Trinity, the existence of demons, and other orthodox religious propositions. Jefferson also was spared professing these doctrines at the baptisms of his own children because it was the godparents, and not the parents, who recited the baptismal creed.

Jefferson on Jesus Christ and Christianity

Contemporary writer Daniel Boorstin describes Jefferson's relationship to Christianity and Christian morality:

> The pure and simple Christian morality had surely been over-laden by dogma and superstition, but the same was true in Buddhism, Mohammedanism, and all other religions—even as Jefferson and Rush remarked—Atheism. It purified Christianity, could promote moral health in the actual setting of eighteenth century America, that was enough to make the Jeffersonian sympathetic. Jefferson more than once called himself a Christian—"a real Christian"—that is, an adherent of the morality of Jesus.[21]

Jefferson's friend David Rittenhouse called himself a Christian, Benjamin Rush was an outspoken Christian, and his mentor Joseph Priestly warned against any one denomination claiming the exclusivity of what is called Christian.

Again, Daniel Boorstin writes:

> The hope that the major problems of life would be solved directly out of experiences of the sensible world was revealed in the whole Jeffersonian approach to Christianity (which was primarily historical); and especially in the active and reformist role assigned to Jesus. The Jeffersonian had projected his own qualities and limitations into Jesus, whose career became his vivid symbol of the superfluity and perils of speculative philosophy. He credited Jesus and the Apostles with an admirably practical, simple, and intelligible morality, growing out of everyday experience. Against them he saw pitted the theologians and metaphysicians.[22]

Thomas Jefferson makes dozens of references to Jesus and to Christianity in his letters and other works. In general, when referring to Jesus or Christianity, Jefferson invariably does so to arrive at a number of conclusions. Among those conclusions are the following. First, that Jesus was the greatest of all moral philosophers. Second, that the teachings of

Jesus have been corrupted, principally at the hands of the early church fathers. Chief among these corrupters were the followers of Plato and the Christian clergy. Third, that these corrupted forms of Christianity eventually will become obsolete. We will take each of these three claims in turn, in the hopes of developing a fuller understanding of Jefferson's view of Christianity.

In regards to Jefferson believing that Jesus was the greatest of all moral teachers, Jefferson wrote in one of his letters:

> But the greatest of all the reformers of the depraved religion of his own country, was Jesus of Nazareth.[23]

In another letter to William Canby from September 18, 1813, Jefferson repeats the claim that Jesus was the greatest of moral teachers. Jefferson tells Canby:

> Of all the systems of morality, ancient or modern, which have come under my observation, none appear to be so pure as that of Jesus.[24]

In speaking of Jefferson's lofty views of Jesus, Charles Sanford concludes:

> It was the life, character, and teachings of the greatest man of all, Jesus Christ, that Jefferson saw the highest attributes of God. He often praised the "pure, simple" teachings of Jesus of "love for only God, and He all perfect." He saw the ministry of Jesus as an attempt to reform the Jewish religion of the evil attributes of God taught by Moses, and to substitute those of the "perfect Supreme Being," which, Jefferson said, Jesus took from "the best qualities of the human head and heart, wisdom, justice, and goodness," and added to them power and infinite perfection. In the moral teachings of Christ, Jefferson found "the most sublime morality which has ever fallen from the lips of man."[25]

Although Jefferson saw in Jesus the greatest moral teacher of all time, he also believed that the original teachings of Jesus were corrupted fairly early on. Speaking of the church shortly after the death of Jesus, Jefferson remarks:

> But a short time elapsed after the death of the great reformer of the Jewish religion, before his principles were departed from

by those who professed to be his servants, and perverted into an engine for enslaving mankind, and aggrandizing their oppressors in Church and State.[26]

Again, about the corruption of the teachings of Jesus, Jefferson wrote:

Theologians have so distorted and deformed the doctrines of Jesus, so muffled them in mysticisms, fancies, and falsehood, have caricatured them into forms so monstrous and inconceivable, as to shock Reasonable thinkers.[27]

Not only did Jefferson think the doctrines of Jesus had been corrupted shortly after his death, he also believed this corrupted form of Christianity has been responsible for a whole host of woes:

Millions of innocent men, women, and children, since the introduction of Christianity, have been burnt, tortured, fined, and imprisoned; yet we have not advanced one inch toward uniformity. What has been the effect of coercion? To make one half the world fools and the other half hypocrites. To support roguery and error all over the earth.[28]

Writing about the effect of the early corruption of the teachings of Jesus, in a letter to Moses Robinson from 1801, Jefferson said:

The Christian religion, when divested from the rags in which they [the clergy] have enveloped it, and brought to the original purity and simplicity of its benevolent institutor, is a religion of all others most friendly to, science, and the freest expansion of the human mind.[29]

Not only did Jefferson believe the doctrines of Jesus were corrupted by the early Christian clergy, he also maintained that the followers of Plato were also responsible for the corruption. In a letter to John Adams from July 5, 1814, Jefferson writes of both sources of the corruption:

The Christian priesthood, finding the doctrines of Christ leveled to every understanding, and too plain to need expansion, saw in the mysticism of Plato, materials with which they might build up an artificial system which might, from its indistinctness, admit everlasting controversy, give employment for their order, and introduce it to profit, power, and preeminence.[30]

In addition to Jefferson's beliefs that Jesus was the greatest of moral teachers, and his belief that the teachings of Jesus had been corrupted chiefly by early church clergy and the followers of Plato, Jefferson also maintained that one day this corrupted form of Christianity will be seen as obsolete. Writing to John Adams on April 11, 1823 Jefferson remarks:

> One day the dawn of reason and freedom of thought in the United States will tear down the artificial scaffolding of Christianity. And the day will come when the mystical generation of Jesus, by the Supreme Being and His Father, in the womb of a virgin will be classed with the fable of the generation of Minerva in the brain of Jupiter.[31]

Jefferson believed that the traditional doctrines of Christianity like the Trinity, the divine nature of Jesus, and other orthodox dogmas will one day become obsolete as many other beliefs from the ancient world have become obsolete and outmoded.

Jefferson also believed that not only was Christianity corrupted in its early history, he also claimed that all religions were superstitious and had their origins in mythology. In a letter to Dr. Woods, Jefferson writes:

> I have recently been examining all the known superstitions of the world, and do not find in our particular superstition [Christianity] one redeeming feature. They are all alike, founded upon fables and mythologies.[32]

Nevertheless, despite Christianity being corrupted and the fact that it arose from superstition, he also claimed repeatedly that Christianity was the best form of religion. In a letter from March 23, 1801, Jefferson tells us:

> The Christian religion when divested of the rags in which they [the clergy] have enveloped, and brought to the original purity and simplicity of its Benevolent Institutor, is a religion of all others most friendly to liberty, Science, and the freest expansion of the human mind.[33]

Although Jefferson saw himself against the corruptions of Christianity, and that Christianity is the best form of religion, he was not opposed to the principal teachings of Jesus. In a letter to Benjamin Rush on April 21, 1803, Jefferson comments:

> My views are the result of a life of inquiry and reflection, and very different from the anti-Christian tradition imputed to me by those who know nothing of my opinions. To the corruptions of Christianity I am, indeed, opposed; but not to the general precepts of Jesus himself. I am a Christian in the only sense in which He wished anyone to be; sincerely attached to his doctrines in the preference to others.[34]

Thus, we can conclude this chapter by saying that Thomas Jefferson believed that Christianity was the best religion available to him; he believed Christianity had been corrupted, early on, mostly by the clergy, by Saint Paul and others, and by some followers of Plato in the early centuries of the church.

Jefferson believed that Christianity, like other world religions, is a collection of superstitions founded on fable and mythology. Nevertheless, he considered himself to be a Christian only so far as Jesus would want someone to be his disciple. The principal beliefs among Jesus and his followers that Jefferson was chiefly attracted to were a host of moral claims about virtue, the nature of moral goodness, and the innate character of moral sense.

A fourth issue where Jefferson makes frequent comments about the teachings of Jesus and Christianity are various attempts by people in Jefferson's day to claim that America is a Christian nation. He also wrote several times about a national day of prayer. It is to these two issues we now wish to turn, so that we might have a fuller understanding of Jefferson's views on Jesus and Christianity.

Jefferson on Christianity, a National Religion, and a Day of Prayer

In Jefferson's autobiography, he suggests that at the time of the writing of the Constitution, some people wished that the words "Jesus Christ" be inserted in the preamble. Jefferson describes the situation:

> Where the preamble declares, that coercion is a departure of the
> Holy Author of our religion, an amendment was proposed by in-
> serting "Jesus Christ," so that it would read "A departure from the
> plan of Jesus Christ, the holy author of our religion." The inser-
> tion was rejected by the great majority, in proof that they meant
> to comprehend, within the mantle of its protection, the Jew and
> the Gentile, the Christian and Mohammedan, the Hindoo and
> Infidel of every denomination.[35]

Jefferson's opinions about the United States not being a Christian
nation were shared by many of the other founders as well. Article 11 of
the *Treaty of Tripoli*, for example, was written during the administration
of George Washington and signed into law by John Adams. Article 11
reads, "The government of the United States is not in any sense founded
on the Christian religion."[36]

The treaty was authored by American diplomat Joel Barlow in 1796.
It was sent to the floor of the U.S. Senate on June 7, 1797, where it was
read aloud in its entirety and unanimously approved.

Article VI, section 3 of the Constitution suggests:

> ...no religious test shall ever be required as a qualification to any
> office or public trust under the United States.[37]

And the First Amendment of the U.S. Constitution declares,
"Congress shall make no law respecting an establishment of religion."[38]
James Madison, in introducing the Bill of Rights at the First Federal
Congress on June 8, 1789, also confirmed that the United States is not
a Christian nation.

Jefferson, as well as many of the other founding fathers and members of the First Congress agreed that the United States would not be
known as a Christian nation. A similar view on a national day of prayer
was also held by Jefferson and James Madison that such proclamations
were violations of the constitutional separation of church and state.

Indeed, Jefferson refused to issue prayer proclamations during his
two terms in the White House. Writing to Samuel Miller on January
23, 1808, Jefferson said, "Fasting and prayer are religious exercises; the
enjoining them an act of discipline. Every religious society has the right
to determine for itself the times for these exercises, and the object proper
for them, according to their own particular tenets; and this right can

never be safer than in their own hands, where the constitution has deposited it."[39]

Four years earlier, in 1802, Jefferson had made the same response to a request from the Danbury Baptists for a national day of fasting. Historian Joyce Appleby describes the request and Jefferson's response:

> In January, 1802, Jefferson had another opportunity to elaborate his take on the Constitution, this time marching into the thorny thicket of state-church relations. The Danbury Baptist Association of Connecticut conveyed to him their delight at his election and requested that he declare a day of fasting to speed the nation's recovery from the acrimony of the recent presidential campaign.[40]

Appleby continues:

> With alacrity, Jefferson turned the Baptists down. This was the occasion he had been waiting for. His response became his most resonate statement about the Constitution, an eighty-three word sentence that confidently asserted that the first amendment had built "a wall of separation between church and state."[41]

James Madison also considered prayer proclamations to be inappropriate. Although he did issue a few "prayer day" proclamations while president, they came under Congressional pressure. Later, Madison said that such proclamations are inappropriate. In his *Detached Memorandum*, Madison wrote that prayer days by government proclamation "seem to imply and certainly nourish the erroneous idea of a national religion."[42]

In short, Jefferson, Madison, and other founding fathers never conceived of the United States as a Christian nation. Nor did they think that the government could make religious pronouncements like a national day of prayer or fasting. Jefferson was very clear about his views on both matters, and these views go into the making of our third president's view of Christianity.

Jefferson also refused to declare a day of Thanksgiving Prayer. Writing to Levi Lincoln on January 1, 1802, he says:

> I have long wished to find, of sayings why I do not proclaim fastings and thanksgivings, as my predecessors did. The address, to be sure, does not point at this, and its introduction is awkward.

> But I see no opportunity to do it more pertinently. I know it will
> give great offense to the New England clergy; but the advocate
> of religious freedom is to expect neither peace nor forgiveness
> from them.[43]

In a correspondence to Rev. Samuel Miller on January 23, 1808,
Jefferson again discusses prayer proclamations:

> I duly received your favor of the eighteenth, and am thankful to
> you for having written it, because it is more agreeable to prevent
> than to refuse what I do not think myself authorized to comply
> with. I consider the government of the United States as inter-
> dicted by the Constitution from intermeddling with religious
> institutions, their doctrines, disciplines, or exercises, which the
> Constitution has directly precluded from them.[44]

Thus, Jefferson was staunchly against both the notion that the
United States is a Christian nation, and the proclamation of national
days of prayer and fasting. Jefferson's basis for being contrary to both of
these propositions was the Constitution.

In chapter six of this work, we conduct a further analysis of the
religious and moral propositions of Jesus that Jefferson was fully in con-
gruence. It is enough now to conclude that Jefferson saw himself as a
Christian, only in so far as he was a follower of Jesus' moral teachings.
Principal among these are the love of God and the Golden Rule.

In addition to following these teachings of Jesus, Thomas Jefferson
also believed that the sense of morality was innate. It is lodged in all
human hearts, and is the same for all humans in every age. Writing to
James Fishback on September 27, 1809, Jefferson discusses this innate
knowledge:

> Reading, reflection, and time convinced me that the interests of
> society require the observation of those moral precepts only in
> which all religions agree (for all forbid us to murder, steal, plun-
> der, or bear false witness), and that we should not intermeddle
> with the particular dogmas in which all religions differ, and
> which are totally unconnected with morality. In all of them we
> see good men, as many in one as another.[45]

Again, we discuss this belief that the human moral sense is innate at length in chapter six, along with a more detailed discussion of the moral teachings of Jesus of Nazareth.

Another idea of Jefferson's that is discussed at length in chapter six is the view that reason and social utility should be the measure of the usefulness of religious beliefs. Jefferson makes this point over and over in his letters, his speeches, and in his published works. When writing about why sea shells would be found in higher elevations than one should reasonably expect, in the *Notes on the State of Virginia*, Jefferson wrote, "Ignorance is preferable to error; and he is less remote from the truth who believes nothing than he who believes what is wrong."[46]

In a 1797 letter to James Sullivan, Jefferson says, "Our principles are founded on the immovable basis of equal right and reason."[47] And in his First Inaugural Address on March 4, 1801, Jefferson proclaimed:

> All, too, will bear in mind this sacred principle, that though the will of the majority is in all cases to prevail, that will, to be rightful, must be reasonable; that the minority possess their equal rights, which equal laws must protect, and to violate which would be oppression.[48]

Conclusions

Several major conclusions can now be made in this chapter. First, Thomas Jefferson was baptized into the Anglican Church, and appears to have remained a member of that church until early adulthood. Jefferson may, or may not, have experienced a religious awakening of sorts, a period of religious crisis, in his years at William and Mary. By early adulthood, Jefferson had refused to be the godfather for the baptism of the children of friends, which would seem to indicate that by the time he finished his law training, Jefferson no longer assented to many of the traditional doctrines of the Anglican Church. Chief among the doctrines that Jefferson rejected were the belief in the Trinity, the divine nature of Jesus, original sin, and the existence of demons.

A second major conclusion made in this chapter is that although Jefferson did not ascribe to himself membership in any Christian church in his adult life, he did, nevertheless, refer to himself in several places as a Christian. Whenever Jefferson refers to himself as a Christian, it is always with some qualification. The principal qualification is that Jefferson calls himself a follower of the doctrines of Jesus. By this he means chiefly the moral teachings of Jesus.

A third conclusion we can make in this chapter is that Thomas Jefferson was against the notion that the United States is a Christian nation, and the proclamation of presidential days of prayer and fasting. Jefferson was contrary to both these ideas due to his view of the Constitution.

A fourth conclusion we may come to in this chapter is that Jefferson believed that the Christian religion, early on, was corrupted in the first 300 years of Christianity. Chief among the corrupters, in Jefferson's view, were Saint Paul, some early church fathers, and second and third century Platonists.

A final conclusion we have made in this chapter is that Thomas Jefferson believed that the moral sense was innate. He believed that God wrote it in the heart of every person, and that the sense of morality is universal and inevitable.

If we may now answer the question posed at the head of this chapter, it is best to say that Thomas Jefferson was a member of the Christian church until his early adulthood. After that period, nowhere does Jefferson claim membership in any Christian church. This may have been due to his not wanting to arm his enemies, or it may be because he could no longer assent to certain traditional doctrines of the Christian church.

While publicly Jefferson did not join as a member of a Christian denomination, privately, Jefferson corresponded with close friends about his religious and moral beliefs, many of which were consistent with the Deists and the Unitarians. Jefferson also privately communicated to friends that he considered himself as a Christian in the sense that he was a believer in the moral teachings of Jesus.

In the final two chapters of this work, we raise two final fundamental questions. What did Thomas Jefferson not believe in? And, what did Thomas Jefferson believe in? The first of these is taken up in chapter five. The second question, we examine in chapter six.

Notes

1. Thomas Jefferson, *The Autobiography of Thomas Jefferson, 1743–1790*, ed. Paul Leicester Ford (Philadelphia: University of Pennsylvania Press, 2005).

2. Ibid.

3. Lyon Gardiner Tyler, "Education in Colonial Virginia," *William and Mary College Quarterly Historical Magazine* 6 (July, 1897) 1–6. Also see, Henry S. Randall, *The Life of Thomas Jefferson* Volume II, 192.

4. Thomas Jefferson, *Autobiography*.

5. Rev. Jonathan Boucher, *Reminiscences of an American Loyalist, 1738–1789* (Boston and New York, 1925) 60–62.

6. James Maury, *A Dissertation on Education in the Form of a Letter from James Maury to Robert Jackson*, July 17, 1762, in *Papers of the Albermale Historical Society* Volume II, 1942, edited by Helen Duprey Bullock.

7. Thomas Jefferson, Letter to John Harvie, January 14, 1760.

8. Thomas Jefferson, Letter to John Trunbull, February 15, 1789.

9. Ibid.

10. From a lecture given by Professor John Fauvel at the University of Virginia, April 15, 1999.

11. Thomas Jefferson, *Autobiography*.

12. Dumas Malone, *Jefferson and the Rights of Man* (Boston: Little Brown, 1951) 83.

13. Charles Sanford, *The Religious Life of Thomas Jefferson* (Charlottsville: University of Virginia Press, 1984) 7.

14. Ibid., 8.

15. Dumas Malone, *Jefferson and the Rights of Man* (Boston: Little Brown, 1951); Henry W. Foote, *Thomas Jefferson: Champion of Religious Freedom, Advocate of Christian Morals* (Boston, 1947); Henry S. Randall, *The Life of Thomas Jefferson* 3 volumes (New York, 1858); James Truslow Adams, *Jefferson Principles and Hamilton Principles* (Boston, 1932); and Henry Cabot Lodge, *History of the United States During the Administration of Thomas Jefferson* (New York: Library of America, 1986).

16. Thomas Jefferson, Letter to Peter Carr, August 10, 1787.

17. Ibid.

18. Ibid.

19. Sanford, 8.

20. *Jefferson's Literary Commonplace Book* Edited by Douglas L. Wilson in *The Papers of Thomas Jefferson*, Second Series (Princeton: Princeton University Press, 1989). Many eighteenth-century college students kept "commonplace books," notebooks in which they copied favorite passages from literary or philosophical works. Jefferson kept commonplace books from 1758 (when he was 15) until 1773, when he was 30. Jefferson treasured this chronicle from his young childhood for the remainder of his life.

21. Daniel Boorstin, *The Lost World of Thomas Jefferson* (Chicago: University of Chicago Press, 1993) 156–57.

22. Ibid., 157.

23. Thomas Jefferson, Letter to John Adams, May 5, 1817.

24. Thomas Jefferson, Letter to William Canby, September 18, 1813.

25. Sanford, 105.

26. Thomas Jefferson, Letter to Thomas Cooper, February 10, 1814.

27. Thomas Jefferson, Letter to Thomas Ritchie, January 21, 1816.

28. Thomas Jefferson, *Notes on Virginia.*

29. Thomas Jefferson, Letter to Moses Robinson, March 23, 1801.

30. Thomas Jefferson, Letter to John Adams, July 5, 1814.

31. Thomas Jefferson, Letter to John Adams, April 11, 1823.

32. Thomas Jefferson to Gordon Woods, September 11, 1802.

33. Thomas Jefferson to Benjamin Rush, March 23, 1801.

34. Thomas Jefferson to Benjamin Rush, April 23, 1803.

35. Thomas Jefferson, *Autobiography.*

36. Joel Barlow, *Treaty of Tripoli*, Article VI, Section 3 (June 7, 1797).

37. Ibid.

38. United States *Constitution.*

39. Thomas Jefferson, Letter to Samuel Miller, January 23, 1808.

40. Joyce Appleby, *Thomas Jefferson* (New York: Henry Holt, 2002) 58.

41. Ibid.

42. James Madison, "Detached Memorandum," in *The Papers of James Madison*, ed. William T. Hutchinson et al., vol. 12 (Charlottesville: University of Virginia Press, 1979) 198.

43. Thomas Jefferson, Letter to Levi Lincoln, January 1, 1802.

44. Thomas Jefferson, Letter to Samuel Miller, January 23, 1808.

45. Thomas Jefferson, Letter to James Fishback, September 27, 1809.

46. Thomas Jefferson, *Notes on the State of Virginia.*

47. Thomas Jefferson, Letter to James Sullivan, February 9, 1797.

48. Thomas Jefferson, *First Inaugural Address*, March 4, 1801.

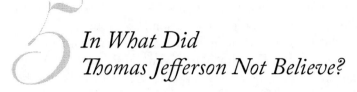

In What Did
Thomas Jefferson Not Believe?

Jefferson here seems to deny the existence of God and of human immortality. But he was not willing to go that far; instead, he decided that both God and the human soul were, in some sense, material.

—Charles B. Sanford
  The Religious Life of Thomas Jefferson

These are the false shepherds foretold as to enter not by the door into the sheep fold, but to climb up some other way. They are mere usurpers of the Christian name, teaching a counter religion made up of the deliria of crazy imaginations.

—Thomas Jefferson
  Letter to Benjamin Waterhouse
  June 26, 1822

He [Jesus] has been enveloped by jugglers to make money of Him, when the genuine character shall be exhibited, which they have dressed up in the rags of an imposter. The world, I say, will at length see the eternal merit of this first of human sages.

—Thomas Jefferson
  Letter to F. A. Van der Kemp
  April 25, 1816

Introduction

FROM CHAPTERS ONE through four of this work, we can glean a collection of Christian doctrines that Jefferson did not believe in. Among these were the Trinity, the dual natures of Jesus, and original sin. These conclusions come chiefly from Jefferson's encounters with Deism, atheism, and the Unitarians, as well as with his enemies, the Christian clergy and the Federalists. Another way to understand what Jefferson thought about the doctrines of traditional Christianity is to look carefully at two works where Jefferson wrote about Jesus. While Jefferson was president, he made a study of the four gospels. Jefferson revised this study some years later. The resulting publication is known as the Jefferson Bible. In addition to these two studies on Jesus, Jefferson also wrote one long essay, and many shorter accounts of Jesus in letters to friends. The long essay appears in a letter to William Short from April 13, 1820. As we shall see, Jefferson mentions his views on Jesus in many letters to John Adams, Benjamin Rush, William Short, and Joseph Priestly.

In this chapter, we hope to do several things. First, carefully to look at Jefferson's writings on Jesus, more fully to understand his view of the founder of Christianity. Second, we will look at those passages that Jefferson incised from the gospels, so that we might have a better handle on which were the teachings to which Jefferson could not assent. In a third section in this chapter, we will look specifically at some other ideas in the Christian tradition that Jefferson rejected. In a fourth section, we discuss some theological issues about which Thomas Jefferson appears to have been quite ambivalent. Finally, we shall make a number of general conclusions about those Christian beliefs that Thomas Jefferson rejected, so that we might answer the question posed in the title of this chapter.

Jefferson on Jesus

Jefferson wrote two major works on the life and teachings of Jesus. The first of these, "A Syllabus of an Estimate of the Merit of the Doctrines of Jesus, Compared With Those of Others," was completed in 1802, during Jefferson's second term in the White House.[1] In this study, Jefferson was interested in comparing the moral teachings of Jesus with those of other ancient writers. It is likely that Jefferson became interested in this project after he had read Joseph Priestly's *Socrates and Jesus Compared,*[2] which concluded that both Socrates and Jesus were heroic moral teachers, but Jesus had the better moral vision.

Jefferson wrote Priestly about his book and suggested he would like to see a study comparing Jesus' ethics to those of Cicero and Seneca, as well as that of the Old Testament. The by-product of this desire was the *Syllabus.*

The origins of the *Syllabus* go back to an 1800 letter from Jefferson to Benjamin Rush in which Jefferson writes, "I promised you a letter on

Christianity, which I have not forgotten. It is because I have reflected on it, that I find much more time necessary for it that I can presently dispose of."[3]

Three years later, Jefferson finally completed the *Syllabus* which arose in the context of another letter that Jefferson wrote to Benjamin Rush on April 21, 1803. In this letter Jefferson says he wishes to outline his view of Jesus. Appended to this letter was the *Syllabus*.[4]

In the letter to Rush, Jefferson says:

> But while this Syllabus is meant to place the character of Jesus in its true light, as no imposter Himself, but a great reformer of the Hebrew code of religion.[5]

In the *Syllabus*, Jefferson comments on Greek philosophers, the religion of the ancient Jews, which Jefferson thought was Deism, and compares the ethical teachings of Jesus with Socrates, Plato, and Epictetus. Moreover, Jefferson also describes in the *Syllabus* what he calls "the intrinsic merits of his doctrines." Chief among these intrinsic doctrines are four, in which Jefferson recounts 1) Jesus corrected the Deism of the Jews; 2) His moral doctrines, love, charity, and peace, are his most important; 3) Jesus "pushed his scrutinizes into the heart of man; erected his tribunal in the region of his thoughts, and purified the waters at the fountain head." And 4) He

> taught emphatically, the doctrines of the future state, which was either doubted or disbelieved by the Jews, and wielded it with efficacy as an important incentive, supplementary to the other motives to the moral conduct.[6]

Jefferson sent the *Syllabus* to Benjamin Rush, and Rush in May of 1803 responded to the *Syllabus*. Rush wrote that he read the *Syllabus* "with great attention."[7] And he "was much pleased to find you are by no means as heterodox as you have been supposed by your enemies."[8] Rush went on in the letter to suggest that his view of Jesus is different from that of Jefferson's. Rush added, "We will agree to disagree."[9]

Jefferson also sent the *Syllabus* to Joseph Priestly on April 24, 1803.[10] Priestly responded to Jefferson a month later in May of 1803. Edwin Gaustad describes Priestly's response:

> Priestly responded to the *Syllabus* the following May in some amazement that Jefferson should deny that Jesus claimed to be on a divine mission. That opinion, Priestly commented somewhat sharply, was one "that I do not remember ever to have heard before."[11]

Priestly found the gospel narratives, as well as the testimonies of the early church fathers to be evidence enough that Jesus was indeed on a divine mission. If Jesus were not on a divine mission, then Priestly concluded, "the whole of subsequent history" becomes "consistent and natural" and of no other hypothesis whatsoever can this be said.[12]

Six months later, Priestly informed Jefferson that he was going to expand his comparison of Socrates and Jesus. Jefferson replied enthusiastically, and commented that "you are so much in possession of the whole subject that you will do it better and easier than any other person living."[13] But Priestly's health had begun to fail, and the Unitarian scientist was dead by February of 1804.

When the news of Priestly's death reached Jefferson on February 16, 1804, Jefferson immediately set to work distilling and refining the *Syllabus*. The result of this distilling and refinement of the moral teachings of Jesus became Jefferson's second work on the first century Jewish sage.

Jefferson's second work on Jesus was called "The Philosophy of Jesus of Nazareth," and was what Jefferson called "an abstract from the Evangelists of whatever has the stamp of the eloquence and fine imagination of Jesus."[14] It was completed in 1816, fourteen years after the *Syllabus*. Jefferson tells us that the *Philosophy of Jesus* was made by "cutting the text out of a book, and arranging them on the page of a blank book, in a certain order of time or subject."[15] The purpose of the *Philosophy* Jefferson told John Adams was to separate "diamonds in a dunghill."[16] In a letter to William Short, Jefferson wrote that he found on the one hand "many passages of fine imagination, correct morality, and of the most lovely benevolence." But all that beauty sat trapped in "so much ignorance, so much absurdity, so much untruth, charlatanism and imposture." Jefferson says he found the work "obvious and easy."[17]

In an 1815 letter to Charles Clay, Jefferson wrote that he "had taken the four Evangelists" and "cut out from them every text they had recorded of the moral precepts of Jesus." Jefferson continues:

and arranged them in a certain order, and although they appeared but as fragments, yet fragments of the most sublime edifice of morality which had ever been exhibited.[18]

Jefferson mentions *The Philosophy of Jesus* in a few other letters, but for the most part he kept the project private, probably guessing that the established churches would see this effort as one more example of his atheism or Deism. Nor did Jefferson care to give his Federalist opponents another reason to question his religious orthodoxy.

Jefferson's redaction of the gospels was also a retaliatory act, as much as anything else, against priests and ministers, "soothsayers and necromancers" as Jefferson called them.

The original version of the *Philosophy of Jesus*, which did not survive, was probably done in English, for Jefferson says he hastily compiled it in "two or three nights only." Later, he wrote that he intended to "add to my little book the Greek, Latin, and French" versions of the gospels, along with the English in four parallel columns. This is precisely the version that has come down to us. It was passed down from heir to heir, until finally, *The Philosophy of Jesus* came into the possession of the Smithsonian in 1895. It was later published by the Government Printing Office in 1904. A study of Jefferson's two versions of the gospels indicates what of Jesus' teachings Jefferson retained, as well as what he rejected.[19]

Jefferson sent a copy of the *Syllabus* to John Adams in 1813. He remarked that this "skeleton" still needed to be supplied, "with arteries, with veins, with nerves, muscles, and flesh." Jefferson added, "that task is beyond my time and information."[20] Six or seven years later, "The Philosophy of Jesus" was Jefferson's attempt to flesh out his remarks in the *Syllabus*. In modern scholarship on Jefferson the "Philosophy of Jesus" is known as the Jefferson Bible. It was originally published by an act of Congress in 1904. The best contemporary version of the Jefferson Bible is the edition published by Princeton University Press in 1983.

The Contents of the Jefferson Bible

The Jefferson Bible begins with the birth of Jesus. Jefferson draws mostly from Luke's gospel; but immediately Jefferson begins an account of Mary and Joseph on their way to Bethlehem; but he omits all of the first chapters' accounts of conversations and announcements from angels. Similarly, Jefferson excised Herod's ordering of the slaying of male children under the age of two.

Following Luke's account, Jefferson keeps the babe "born in swaddling clothes, and laid in a manger," but he removed the appearance of an angel to the shepherds watching over their flocks, as well as the heavenly host singing "Glory to God in the highest."[21]

In Jefferson's version of the gospels, he moves quickly from the babe in swaddling clothes to circumcision on the eighth day, and then follows it quickly by Jesus' visit to the Temple in Jerusalem at about age twelve. In the Luke account, when his parents inquire where their son has been, Jesus replies "I must be about my father's business." Luke adds: "And they did not understand what he had said to them." Apparently, Jefferson did not understand it as well, for he dropped the entire story.[22]

The second chapter of Luke ends with: "And Jesus grew in wisdom and stature, and in favor with God and man." Jefferson simply uses the words, "And Jesus grew in wisdom and stature." When Jefferson got to the beginning of the third chapter of Luke, Jefferson passed over the reference to Jesus preaching a baptism of repentance for the forgiveness of sins. Jefferson included the baptism of Jesus, but he excised anything about the heavens opening up, or the spirit of God "descending like a dove,"[23] and the voice from heaven saying, "This is my son, in whom I am well pleased."[24]

Jefferson also omits Luke's genealogy in Luke 3:23–38, as well as all four gospel accounts of Jesus' temptation by the Devil in the wilderness for forty days and forty nights. In John's account of the wedding feast at Cana, Jefferson removed the turning of water into wine. Jefferson also excises the feeding of the 5,000 in his version of the gospel of John, as well as Jesus walking on water in chapter six of John's gospel.

Jefferson's treatment of the Sermon on the Mount is also curious. He presents the beatitudes in Matthew's version (5:1–12), then switches to Luke's woes (6:24–26), and then abruptly switches back to Matthew 5, which he follows to the end. But Jefferson deleted "Be perfect, even as your father in heaven is perfect," while preferring Luke's line about loving one's enemies and doing good, as well as "Be merciful, as your father in heaven is also merciful."[25]

At this point in the Jefferson Bible, the President gives Matthew's account of almsgiving in chapter six, along with the Lord's prayer, the treasures in heaven, and the lilies of the field homily that concludes the episode.

Jefferson includes Matthew chapter seven and its moral instructions, including "whatever you should will that men do to you do to them, for this is the law of the prophets."[26] The end of chapter seven of Matthew veers off into a discussion of heavenly things, salvation, and damnation (Matthew 7:21–23). Jefferson omits these verses, and replaces them with a story from Matthew 12:35–37, about good trees bearing good fruit.

Jefferson then returns to chapter seven of Matthew, where a wise man built his house not upon sand, but upon rock. Jefferson then jumps from one to another of the four gospels, citing the passages that include Jesus' most important moral teachings; but along the way, Jefferson deletes the miracles of Jesus and his raisings from the dead.

Jefferson includes most of chapter twelve of Luke, but omits the few verses that speak of angels. Jefferson also excises all four resurrection accounts of Jesus. The Jefferson Bible also deletes any accounts that refer to Jesus' divinity. Jefferson's account also contains no appearances of Jesus after the resurrection, and no ascension into heaven.

Thus Jefferson seemed primarily interested in deleting from the gospels any references to angels, Jesus' miracles, souls and spirits, as well as any mention of resurrection of the body. The rejection of these beliefs, plus what we have said earlier in this study about Jefferson on the Trinity and the divine nature of Jesus, is the core of Christian beliefs that Jefferson rejected.

The Jefferson Bible ends with the words, "Now, in the place where he was crucified, there was a garden, and in the garden a new sepulcher."[27] Jefferson continues:

> wherein was never man yet laid. There laid them Jesus. And rolled
> a great stone to the door of the sepulcher, and departed.[28]

Jefferson uses the end of chapter 19 of John's gospel, but he leaves out the appearance to Mary Magdalene, the appearance to the disciples, the appearance in Galilee, and the instructions to Peter and John. From chapter 24 of Luke, Jefferson removes the story on the road to Emmaus, the appearance of Jesus' disciples, and the Ascension.

From Matthew's gospel, Jefferson excises the story of the guard at the tomb, the report of the guard, and the commissioning of the disciples. From the Mark account, Jefferson removes the appearances to Mary Magdalene, and to the two disciples, as well as Jesus' commission to the disciples and the Ascension. Indeed, Jefferson removes all four accounts of Jesus' resurrection, and any post-crucifixion appearances.

Other Ideas Rejected by Jefferson

In addition to the beliefs mentioned above, Jefferson rejected a number of other central beliefs of traditional Christianity. He rejected, for example, what he called the "five demoralizing dogmas of Calvin," which he believed included belief in the Trinity and original sin. Jefferson wrote in several letters his opposition to predestination and eternal damnation, calling them "incomprehensible faith that denies the use of reason in religion."[29] Jefferson adapted Conyers Middleton's view that the story of the fall of man in Genesis three is "a fable or allegory."[30]

Jefferson also regularly attacked St. Paul, chiefly because it was Paul from whom Calvin developed his theology. Jefferson believed that Paul was among the first of the corruptors of the authentic message of Jesus, and saw him as the inventor of salvation by grace and original sin, two ideas he was staunchly against.

Eugene Sheridan, in writing about Jefferson's view of original sin, says this:

> No less absurd was the Christian plan of redemption and the doctrine of the fall of man upon which it was predicated. In regard to the latter, it was "in all circumstances, absolutely irreconcilable that a just God sent his only begotten son, who had not offended him, to be sacrificed by men, who had offended him, that he might expiate this sin, and satisfy his own anger."[31]

It was from Bolingbroke that Jefferson got the idea of rejecting the fall and redemption. Bolingbroke said that Jesus did not redeem the world because Jesus was not God.

Writing about Paul's influence on early Christianity, Jefferson wrote:

> Christianity . . . (has become) the most perverted system that was ever shown on earth . . . Rogueries, absurdities, and untruths were perpetrated upon the teachings by a large band of dupes

and imposters led by Paul, the great corrupter of the teachings of Jesus.[32]

In addition to rejecting the letters of Paul, Jefferson also had considerable doubts about other books in the New Testament. The principal one is Revelation. Indeed, Jefferson says of the book it is "merely the ravings of a maniac, no more worthy nor capable of explanation than the incoherence of our own nightly dreams."[33]

In a letter to William Short dated October 31, 1819, Jefferson spells out his view of several central Christian doctrines. He cites:

> the immaculate conception of Jesus, his deification, the creation of the world by him, his miraculous powers, his resurrection and visible ascension, his corporeal presence in the Eucharist, the Trinity, original sin, atonement, regeneration, election, orders of hierarchy, etc.[34]

All these ideas, Jefferson suggests, were "artificial systems, invented by Ultra-Christian sects, unauthorized by any single word ever uttered by Jesus."[35] As we have argued earlier in this work, Jefferson believed these issues of faith were deliberately fabricated by the clergy, by Paul, and by followers of Platonic philosophy in the first few hundred years of Christianity.

In the same letter to Short, Jefferson expressed his debt to the "labor and learning" of Priestly for his theological views. Indeed, the Virgin Birth occupies a good portion of *The Corruptions of Christianity*.[36] Priestly also pointed out that the traditional Jewish conception of the Messiah was that a great man would come from the family of David, not a man who is also a God. Priestly also attributed the idea that Jesus was divine to some second century Christian writers. Priestly contended that the corruption of Christianity came at the hands of Platonists, philosophers who believed Jesus' message of eternal life. In all these beliefs, Jefferson followed Priestly closely.

In addition to the ideas mentioned above, Jefferson also rejected the traditional view of the scriptures. His rejection of scripture came primarily in three different ways. First, Jefferson rejected the idea that scripture was divinely inspired. Jefferson believed the Bible was written by humans, and it has all the contradictions and foibles of humans.

Secondly, Jefferson believed that many of the stories of the Old Testament were to be understood as fables or allegories, and not as historical truth. And finally, Jefferson was against the idea that many of the miraculous tales of the Bible, whether it is Moses parting the Red Sea or Jesus bringing Lazarus back from the dead, were against the laws of nature and reason. These miraculous events could not have occurred the way the Bible says they did because, in Jefferson's view, they are impossible.

Jefferson believed that children should be introduced to the Bible early on, in much the same way he was read to from the scriptures as a small child. In writing to John Adams, Jefferson specifically discusses the education of children in biblical matters:

> Instead, therefore, of putting the Bible and the Testament into the hands of children at an age when their judgments are not sufficiently matured for religious inquiries, their memories may here be stored with the most useful facts from Grecian, Roman, European, and American history.[37]

Jefferson suggests in the same letter that the earliest understandings of morality also should be inculcated at this early stage:

> The first element of morality too may be instilled into their minds; such as, when further developed as the judgments advance in strength, may teach them how to work out their greatest happiness, by showing them that it does not depend on the condition of life in which chance has placed them, but is always the result of good conscience, good health, occupation, and freedom in all pursuits.[38]

Thus, Jefferson appears not to have believed in a number of traditional tenets of the Christian church. Among the doctrines Jefferson rejected were the Trinity, the divinity of Jesus, original sin, the atonement, the damnation of souls, transubstantiation, the immaculate conception, and the resurrection of Jesus. There are also a few theological issues about which Jefferson seems to have been ambivalent. We will deal with these issues in the next section of this chapter.

Jefferson and the Clergy

In addition to the beliefs mentioned above rejected by Thomas Jefferson, we also have argued in this work that our third president took a very dim view of the clergy in general and certain denominations in particular. As we have shown, Jefferson was of the belief that certain early church fathers were responsible for the corrupting of the Christian church. He believed that these Platonist philosophers, as well as Saint Paul, presented a false set of beliefs as the teachings of Jesus.

We also have shown a number of times in this work that Jefferson was quite pessimistic about the theology of John Calvin in particular and the Presbyterians in general. Jefferson's chief complaint about Calvin was what he called his "five points," which involve the reformer's views of predestination and salvation by faith through grace. In its stead, Jefferson advocated salvation by works.

In his own time, Jefferson also regularly wrote about the clergy—and little of it was positive. He called the clergy "necromancers," "charlatans," and "corruptors of the faith." as we have shown earlier, Jefferson was generally criticized in his own day by the Christian clergy and the President responded in kind. Jefferson was criticized by the Christian clergy before the election of 1800, and throughout his political career. The only clergy he did not criticize were members of the Unitarian faith, chiefly because he held many of the same metaphysical views.

Jefferson was fond of some clergymen in his own life, the Reverend Maury and his friend Jared Sparks, for examples, but he was cautious and critical of other members of the clergy, both in his own life, and in general. In his own life, Jefferson said harsh things about the Reverend William Douglas, the Presbyterian minister who taught Jefferson in his youth; and Jefferson was also critical of national members of the clergy in his own day. Jefferson sums up his view of the clergy in a letter to Horatio Spafford from 1814:

> In every country and every age, the priest has been hostile to liberty. He is always in alliance with the despot, abetting his abuses in return for protection to his own. It is error alone that needs the support of government. Truth can stand by itself.[39]

A final religious belief, then, rejected by Thomas Jefferson is that the Christian clergy plays an important role in the history of the Christian church.

Jefferson's Theologically Ambivalent Beliefs

Of all Jefferson's religious beliefs, he was most ambivalent about immortality. Writing of this ambivalence, Sanford says:

> Of all Jefferson's writings on religious subjects, his comments on life after death have presented the most difficulties to scholars, possibly because the subject itself perplexed Jefferson more than any other ... Most have concluded that his writings on immortality are so contradictory that they will always be subject of controversy.[40]

The theological issue about which Thomas Jefferson was most ambivalent was immortality of the soul. From the available evidence, Jefferson seems to have believed, and to have not believed in the continuing survival of the soul after death. On the negative side of this argument, there are the many proclamations of Jefferson that he was a materialist. On the positive side, are a number of Jefferson's letters where he seems to express belief in immortality of the soul. The most extensive discussion of Jefferson's on immortality is in a dialogue with John Adams in their letters at the end of Jefferson's life. Indeed, it was Adams who first inquired of Jefferson what is meant by "spirit and matter?"[41]

Adams suggests that neither the saint who believes in spirit, nor scientist who thought everything is matter, knew what spirit and matter really are. Jefferson responds by writing, "Your puzzling letter on matter and spirit, with its crowd of skepticism, kept me from sleep."[42] Jefferson continues:

> I read it, laid it down, and then read it again.[43]

But then Jefferson added these lines:

> To talk of immaterial existences is to talk of nothings. To say that the human soul, angels, or God are immaterial is to say they are nothings, or that there are no God, no angels, no soul.[44]

In this letter, Jefferson seems to have accepted Priestly's view of materialism. In referring to the difference between Jesus and himself, Jefferson wrote, "I am a materialist. He takes the side of spiritualism." In a variety of other letters, Jefferson expresses his materialism. And yet, there is another side to Jefferson's view of materialism. In a letter to Thomas Cooper on August 14, 1820, Jefferson wrote:

> Although spiritualism is most prevalent with all these [modern] sects, yet with none of them, I presume, is materialism, declared heretical . . . The fathers of the church of the three first centuries generally, if not universally, were materialists, extending even to the Creator Himself.[45]

Not only did Jefferson believe the church fathers of the first three centuries were materialist, in a letter to Judge Augustus B. Woodward on March 24, 1824, he also suggests that Jesus was a materialist:

> Indeed, Jesus himself, the founder of our religion, was unquestionably a materialist as to man.[46]

Yet, in the same letter Jefferson says, "Jesus said that God is spirit *pneuma*, without defining it."[47]

Jefferson calls himself a materialist, while at the same time, he says in this letter to his college friend John Page that we should live with "pious resignation to the Divine Will until we receive our just reward from God at journey's end."[48] Similarly, in a correspondence to Benjamin Rush on March 6, 1813, Jefferson wished Rush good tidings, "To your health and life here, till you wish to awake to it in another state of being."[49]

This ambivalence about immortality of the soul was a long-standing problem for Thomas Jefferson. While in his first term of office, Jefferson wrote the Rev. Isaac Story on December 5, 1801:

> The laws of nature have withheld from us knowledge of the country of spirits, and left us in the dark, as we were.[50]

Jefferson expresses this same ambiguity in a letter to John Adams, where he wrote:

> I am satisfied and sufficiently occupied with the things which are without tormenting or troubling myself about those which may indeed be, but of which I have no evidence.[51]

Jefferson at the same time seems to be saying that he is a materialist, while also saying that one need not worry or believe anything for which there is not sufficient evidence.

Some modern scholars suggest that Jefferson was not ambivalent about immortality. Edwin Gaustad, for example, tells us in his *Sworn on the Altar of God*:

> Jesus taught "the belief in a future state," and Jefferson endorsed the teaching, for it constituted a central element in his notion of a moral universe.[52]

In addition to Jefferson's ambivalence about immortality of the soul, he was also ambivalent about resurrection of the body. On the one hand, Jefferson was a materialist, and did not believe in the possibility of bringing back people from the dead. On the other hand, Priestly believed in resurrection of the body, and Jefferson may have been leaning in that direction when, in a letter to Augustus Woodward from March 24, 1824, Jefferson wrote about Jesus:

> In all his doctrines of the resurrection, he teaches expressly that the body is to rise in substance. In the Apostles Creed, we all declare that we believe in the "resurrection of the body." Jesus said that God is spirit *pneuma* ... without defining it.[53]

In a letter to Isaac Story, Jefferson admits to having ambivalent feelings about survival after death. He says:

> When I was young, I was fond of the speculations which seemed to promise some insight into that hidden country, but observing that they left me in the same ignorance in which they had found me. I have for many years ceased to read or to think concerning them, and have reposed my head on the pillow of ignorance which a benevolent Creator has made so soft for us, knowing how much we should be forced to use it. I have thought it better, by nourishing the good passions and controlling the bad, to merit an inheritance in a state of being of which I can know so little, and to trust for the future to Him who has been so good for the past.[54]

Jefferson further comments on this ambivalence about the afterlife, when responding in the same letter to the Rev. Isaac Story on December

5, 1801. The Rev. Story had asked what Jefferson believed on the doctrine of transmigration of the soul. Jefferson responds:

> It is not for me to pronounce on the hypothesis you present of a transmigration of souls from one body to another in certain cases. The laws of nature have withheld from us the means of physical knowledge of the country of spirits, and revelation has, for reasons unknown to us, chose to leave us in the dark, as it were.[55]

It is clear that Jefferson's ambivalence about survival after death did not simply involve his views of immortality of the soul, but also his beliefs about resurrection of the body as well.

Finally, Jefferson also displays some ambivalence about his conception of God. The God of the Old Testament is anthropomorphic, stern, and vindictive, while the God of the New Testament is loving and compassionate. Jefferson resolves this ambivalence by preferring the God of the early church over that of the ancient Hebrews.

Jefferson got his idea of finding the God of the Old Testament repugnant from Bolingbroke. Bolingbroke says the deity of the Old Testament was "partial, unjust, and cruel; delights in blood commands, assassinations, massacres, and even extermination of people."[56]

In Bolingbroke's view, this is contrasted with the New Testament where he

> elects some of his creatures to salvation, and predestines others to damnation, even in the womb of their mothers.[57]

Jefferson believed, as Bolingbroke did, that traditional conceptions of God were unacceptable to a rational man because at its heart is a conception of God that is fundamentally contradictory. The conception of God, as seen by Jefferson, is a mystery. As he expresses in his *Commonplace Books*, "No man can believe he knoweth not what nor why."[58]

Scripture and Doctrine in which Jefferson Did Not Believe

For the most part, Jefferson thought the gospels were the inspired word of God. He was not, however, convinced that the writings of Paul were divinely inspired. Jefferson believed that Paul was among the early corruptors of the teachings of Jesus. Indeed, in a correspondence to William

Short, Jefferson wrote, "Paul was the great Coryphaeus, and first corrup-
tor of the doctrines of Jesus."[59]

Jefferson also had doubts about the divine inspiration of many of
the more violent stories in the Old Testament. In addition, Jefferson also
wrote pejoratively about the Book of Revelation. In a correspondence
with Thomas Jefferson Smith, Jefferson remarks:

> No man on earth has less taste or talent for criticisms than my-
> self, and least and last of all should I undertake to criticize works
> on the Apocalypse. It has been fifty or sixty years since I read it,
> and I then considered it as merely the ravings of a maniac, no
> more worthy nor capable of explanation than the incoherence of
> our own nightly dreams.[60]

This comment is an interesting one, when we consider that Jefferson,
in his version of the gospels, kept what is sometimes called the "Little
Apocalypse," of chapters 24 and 25 of Matthew that describes the end
of the world and Jesus' return to the earth. Sanford suggests this is "only
so he could use the account of Jesus judging people from his throne and
separating the good from the bad as a shepherd separates his sheep from
his goats, for he omits the verses that tell of Christ coming down from
heaven with angels."[61]

Jefferson's objections to these apocalyptic passages about the end
of the world are similar to his rejection of the God of wrath found in
the Old Testament, as well as the theology of John Calvin. Jefferson
believed this view of God was based on a low idea of God that derives
from the basest of human emotions. Writing about Calvin's doctrine of
God, Jefferson tells us:

> Calvin's character of this Supreme Being seems chiefly copied
> from that of the Jews.[62]

Presumably, what Jefferson meant by this remark is that the Old
Testament view of God is sometimes a God that is vengeful and wrath-
ful. Jefferson also points out in a letter to Thomas B. Parker on May 15,
1819, that his view of salvation is also contrary to that of Calvin:

> My fundamental principle would be the reverse of Calvin's, that
> we are to be saved by our good works which are within our power,
> and not by our faith which is not without our power.[63]

Jefferson mentions John Calvin and his view of salvation by faith through grace in several of his letters. Jefferson always mentions Calvin in a pejorative way, and when he does, he usually suggests salvation by works as an alternative to salvation by faith through grace. Among the beliefs of traditional Christianity that are rejected by Thomas Jefferson, then, we must include salvation by faith through grace.

It is a curious fact that Jefferson only used the four gospels when constructing the Jefferson Bible. The New Testament contains twenty-three other books besides the gospels. We know from Jefferson's comments about Paul that Paul's letters were corruptions of the doctrines of Jesus. We must also assume that none of the twenty-three books besides the gospels were, in Jefferson's view, divinely inspired. Thus Jefferson read the gospels selectively, picking and choosing what he did and did not see as authentic teachings of Jesus. Jefferson also seems to have little confidence in the twenty-three other books of the New Testament, including the letters of Paul and the letters of Peter, Jude, John, and the other Pastoral Epistles as well.

Jefferson's Views of Established Church

One final religious proposition to which Thomas Jefferson did not assent was the belief that the government should sanction an established church. Jefferson's long-time rejection of this idea can be seen as early as his thoughts when he returned from the Second Continental Congress in 1776, when Jefferson began to make plans to eradicate the "spiritual tyranny" of Virginia's Anglican establishment. Joyce Appleby picks up the story:

> Scouring Virginia's law books for evidence of abusive power, he uncovered statues that empowered magistrates to take away the children of freethinking parents and enjoined imprisonment for those who denied the Trinity. With his usual thoroughness, he spent six years herding those laws toward extinction. Virginia's Quakers, Presbyterians, and Baptists joined forces with Jefferson and other rationalists to strip the Church of England—now called the Episcopal Church—of all the privileges and powers, from which they had long suffered. The Bill for Establishing Religious Freedom declared grandly "that no man shall be compelled to frequent or support any religious worship, place, or min-

istry whatsoever, nor shall he be enforced, restrained, molested, or burdened in his body or goods, nor shall otherwise suffer on account of his religious opinions or beliefs."[64]

When asked directly about his religious views, Jefferson responded, "I am for freedom of religion, and against all maneuvers to bring a legal of one sect over another."[65] Jefferson held this view early on in 1776, and he continued to hold it throughout the remainder of his life. He expressed this view in many of the founding documents of this country, and he also regularly expressed it in letters throughout his adult life. A final theological belief, then, that Thomas Jefferson did not believe in was the view that the state or the government should sanction the establishment of an official church.

Even late in life, Jefferson was engaged in his "crusade against ignorance." Bernard Mayo speaks of Jefferson at the end of his life:

> Looking back to the days when he had struggled to remove legal shackles from men's minds and consciences, he rejoiced that America had become "this blessed land of free inquiry and belief."[66]

Throughout Jefferson's adult life, then, he was diametrically opposed to the establishment of a state church, while remaining optimistic about the exercise of religious freedom throughout the land.

Conclusions

In this chapter, we set out to discuss what traditional Christian theological beliefs Thomas Jefferson did not believe in. In our exploration in this chapter, we may conclude that our third president did not believe in the doctrine of the Trinity, the divinity of Jesus, the miracles of Jesus, the existence of angels and spirits, the virgin birth, original sin, the atonement, transubstantiation, election, predestination, the damnation of souls to hell, that the Old Testament was the word of God, and that 23 of the 27 books of the New Testament were divinely inspired.

We have arrived at these conclusions principally from examining what Jefferson deleted in his *The Philosophy of Jesus of Nazareth*. Most of those deletions, we discovered were related to what we broadly would refer to as "metaphysical issues." Because of Jefferson's materialism, and the influence on his beliefs by Priestly and Bolingbroke, Jefferson concluded that reason would dictate the rejection of angels, miracles, spirits, and other Christian metaphysical beliefs.

We also have suggested in this chapter that Jefferson was ambivalent about a number of other Christian doctrines. Among these are his views of resurrection of the body at the end of time, immortality of the soul, and traditional attributes of God. Jefferson seems to have had mixed feelings about these doctrines, as did his theological mentors Priestly, Bolingbroke, and Shaftesbury.

One conclusion at which we have arrived in this chapter is that Jefferson had a very complicated view of some theological matters. And it was a view that he shared with few people. This may have been due to a worry of what his enemies would say if his books on Jesus were to be made public, or the complexity may have been the product of his internal ambiguity on some theological matters. Or the source of this complexity might be that "Jefferson as Scientist" and "Jefferson as Theologian" are two very different thinkers. Jefferson the scientist was a materialist, and all that implies, while Jefferson the theologian has inherited a number of Christian doctrines that are at odds with materialism. Jefferson had trust in reason and the laws of nature, while at the same time may have had a belief in immortality that seems to contradict those laws. This same ambivalence can be seen in Jefferson's theological mentors, particularly Priestly's views about survival after death.

What is clear is that Jefferson rejected much of traditional Christian doctrine like the Trinity, the dual natures of Jesus, and the miracles of Jesus as they are presented in the gospels. It is also clear from his *Philosophy of Jesus of Nazareth* that he believed in a number of central dogmas in the Christian church. And at the center of Jefferson's view of Christianity are the moral teachings of the man from Nazareth.

We will conclude this chapter with a list of theological beliefs that Jefferson did not believe in, so that we might answer the question at the head of this chapter. Thomas Jefferson did not believe in the following:

1. The Trinity
2. The divinity of Jesus
3. Original sin

4. The atonement

5. Transubstantiation

6. Spirits

7. Angels

8. Salvation by faith through grace

9. Predestination

10. The damning of souls to Hell

11. The second coming

12. The resurrection of Jesus

13. The miracles of Jesus

14. The virgin birth

15. The ascension of Jesus

16. The Old Testament as the Word of God

17. That Jesus was on a divine mission

18. That the God of the OT and the NT are the same God

19. The authority of the letters of Paul

20. Any miraculous events in the OT

21. The more vengeful and stern attributes of God in the Old Testament

22. Demons

23. The authority of the Book of Revelation

24. Apocalyptic passages in the Old and New Testaments

25. An established church

26. That the clergy played a key role in the life of the church

In the sixth and final chapter of this work, we talk more specifically about those things that Jefferson did believe in regarding theological matters. Clearly, one source for determining Jefferson's religious beliefs are carefully to look at those portions of the four gospels that he let remain in his *Philosophy of Jesus of Nazareth*. Other sources for chapter six include Jefferson's *Syllabus*, as well as a number of his letters, where

Jefferson talks positively about his faith. It is to these sources, as well as Jefferson's positive proclamations of his faith that we will now turn in the final chapter of this work.

Notes

1. "Syllabus for the Merits of the Doctrines of Jesus," in *Thomas Jefferson Papers*, Special Collections Department, University of Virginia Library.

2. Joseph Priestly, *Jesus and Socrates Compared* (Whitefish, Mont.: Kessinger, 1997).

3. Thomas Jefferson, Letter to Benjamin Rush, April 21, 1803.

4. Ibid.

5. Ibid.

6. Ibid.

7. Benjamin Rush, Letter to Thomas Jefferson, May 17, 1803.

8. Ibid.

9. Ibid.

10. Thomas Jefferson, Letter to Joseph Priestly, April 24, 1803.

11. Edwin Gaustad, *Sworn on the Altar of God* (Grand Rapids, Michigan: Eerdmans, 1996) 117.

12. Ibid.

13. Ibid., 118.

14. Thomas Jefferson, *The Life and Morals of Jesus of Nazareth* (Washington: Government Printing Office, 1904).

15. Thomas Jefferson, Letter to Benjamin Rush, April 21, 1803.

16. Thomas Jefferson, Letter to William Short, October 31, 1819.

17. Ibid.

18. Thomas Jefferson, Letter to Charles Clay, January 29, 1815.

19. Thomas Jefferson, Letter to James Monroe, January 1, 1815.

20. Allen Jayne, *The Religious and Moral Wisdom of Thomas Jefferson* (New York: Vantage Books, 1984) 97–182.

21. Thomas Jefferson, Letter to John Adams, October 13, 1813.

22. *Life and Morals of Jesus.*

23. Ibid.

24. Ibid.

25. Ibid.

26. Ibid.

27. Ibid.

28. Ibid.

29. Thomas Jefferson, Letter to John Adams, April 11, 1823.

30. Charles Sanford, *The Religious Life of Thomas Jefferson* (Charlottesville: University of Virginia Press, 1984) 62.

31. Eugene Sheridan, *Jefferson and Religion* (Charlottesville: Thomas Jefferson Foundation, 1998) 16.

32. Thomas Jefferson, Letter to William Short, April 13, 1820.

33. Thomas Jefferson, Letter to William Short, October 31, 1819.

34. Ibid.

35. Joseph Priestly, "The Corruption of Christianity," in *Joseph Priestly: Selections From His Writings*, edited by Ira V. Brown (University Park, Pa., 1962).

36. *Notes on the State of Virginia.*

37. Thomas Jefferson, Letter to John Adams, October 14, 1816.

38. Ibid.

39. Thomas Jefferson to Horatio Spafford, March 17, 1814.

40. Sanford, 141.

41. John Adams, Letter to Thomas Jefferson, May 12, 1815.

42. Thomas Jefferson, Letter to John Adams, August 15, 1820.

43. Ibid.

44. Thomas Jefferson, Letter to Thomas Cooper, August 14, 1820.

45. Thomas Jefferson, Letter to Augustus Woodward, March 24, 1824.

46. Ibid.

47. Thomas Jefferson, Letter to John Page, July 15, 1763.

48. Thomas Jefferson, Letter to Benjamin Rush, March 6, 1813.

49. Thomas Jefferson, Letter to Isaac Story, December 5, 1801.

50. Thomas Jefferson, Letter to John Adams, August 5, 1820.

51. Gaustad, 162.

52. Thomas Jefferson, Letter to Augustus Woodward, March 24, 1824.

53. Thomas Jefferson, Letter to Isaac Story, December 5, 1801.

54. Henry Saint John Bolingbroke, quoted in Sanford, 119.

55. Thomas Jefferson, Letter to Isaac Story, December 5, 1801.

56. Sanford, 119.

57. Ibid.

58. *Commonplace Books.*

59. Thomas Jefferson, Letter to William Short, April 13, 1820.

60. Thomas Jefferson, Letter to Thomas Jefferson Smith, February 21, 1825.

61. Sanford, 121–22.

62. Thomas Jefferson, Letter to John Adams, April 11, 1823.

63. Thomas Jefferson, Letter to Thomas B. Parker, May 15, 1819.

64. Joyce Appleby, *Thomas Jefferson* (New York: Henry Holt, 2003) 60.

65. Ibid.

66. Bernard Mayo, *Jefferson Himself* (Charlottsville: University of Virginia Press, 1942) 316.

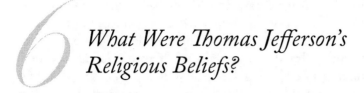

What Were Thomas Jefferson's Religious Beliefs?

I am a real Christian, that is to say, a follower of the doctrines of Jesus.

—Thomas Jefferson
　　Letter to Charles Thompson
　　January 9, 1816

Reason and inquiry are the only effectual agents against terror.

—Thomas Jefferson
　　Letter to Mrs. Harrison Smith
　　August 6, 1816

Belief in the freedom of religion—which to him meant freedom of the mind—lay at the heart of his philosophy and he was always proud to be identified with it.

—Dumas Malone
　　Jefferson and the Rights of Man

Introduction

IN THE FIRST five chapters of this study, we have attempted to ask and answer five principal questions. Was Thomas Jefferson an atheist? Was Thomas Jefferson a Deist? Was Thomas Jefferson a Unitarian? Was Thomas Jefferson a Christian? And, What did Thomas Jefferson not believe in with respect to religion? In terms of the first four questions, we have suggested that he was not an atheist, not a Deist, nor, in his adult life, a member of a Christian church. We also have argued that although Jefferson was attracted to the theology of the Unitarians, nowhere does Jefferson say he is to be numbered among their members.

In regard to whether Jefferson was a Christian, nowhere in his adult life does our third president indicate that he is a member of any Christian church. Although on many occasions Jefferson calls himself a Christian, or a follower of the teachings of Jesus, there is no evidence in his adult life that Jefferson was a member of any Christian denomination.

Henry Stephens Randall suggests that Jefferson regularly attended Anglican church services, using his own well-worn prayer book, but there is no evidence that Jefferson, in his adult life, considered himself a member of the Episcopal Church.[1]

In respect to our fifth question, "What did Jefferson not believe in?," we developed a detailed analysis of those doctrines of the Christian church to which Jefferson could not assent. At the close of chapter five, we provided a list of those propositions, along with evidence, of the doctrines of the Christian church that Jefferson rejected.

In this sixth and final chapter, we focus on four issues. First, we shall make a number of distinctions among several categories of beliefs that Jefferson had concerning religion. Second, we shall explore each of those different categories, providing examples in each of those categories. Third, we will look at a number of places where Thomas Jefferson gave others moral advice. And finally, we shall bring this sixth chapter, and this study in general, to a close by making a list of those religious propositions in which Thomas Jefferson did believe. We then will end the chapter with some general conclusions.

Different Categories of Jefferson's Religious Beliefs

When Thomas Jefferson thought or wrote about religion, it was generally in one of four major categories. The first of those categories is those beliefs that are related to political rights related to religion. The principal ideas in this category are his views on religious freedom, religious toleration, the separation of church and state, and his views of inalienable rights. We shall call this first category "Political Religious Beliefs."

The second category of Jefferson's religious beliefs is related to a group of propositions that, for the most part, were idiosyncratic to Jefferson and a selected few. Among these beliefs of Jefferson were that he thought that religion was a private matter; that religion is best known through reason; that those who labor in the earth are God's chosen people; that the rhythms of the natural world are superior to the values of individuals or societies; that the moral sense is innate; and that those who think they know the most are often the most ignorant.

The third category of Thomas Jefferson's religious beliefs is a collection of thoughts and beliefs that Jefferson shares with traditional Christianity. Among this set of beliefs are that there is one God; that God created the universe; that Jesus was the greatest of moral teachers; and that the cultivation of certain virtues leads to happiness. We shall call this third category, "Traditional Religious Beliefs."

In the fourth and final category of Jefferson's religious beliefs are those that are related to Jesus' moral teachings. The principal evidence for this fourth category is Jefferson's two books about Jesus, the *Syllabus* and the *Philosophy of Jesus of Nazareth*. In this fourth category are specific moral pronouncements that Jefferson believed were straight from Jesus' mouth. We shall call this fourth category, "Moral Beliefs." Of these four categories, the fourth one is the biggest one. It is also the one that most typically reveals Jefferson's moral beliefs. We shall now deal with each of the four categories in turn to sketch more fully Jefferson's religious vision.

Jefferson's Political Religious Beliefs

Thomas Jefferson's political religious beliefs, for the most part, are religious propositions that are related to the founding documents of this country, as well as Jefferson's "Act for Establishing Religious Freedom in Virginia." Among these beliefs are Jefferson's views of religious freedom, religious toleration, and the separation of church and state. Jefferson's views on these matters are sketched out in the U.S. Constitution, the Bill of Rights, the Declaration of Independence, the "Act for Establishing Religious Freedom in Virginia," and in "A Summary View of the Rights of British America."

In his book, *Jefferson's Secrets*, Andrew Burstein speaks of the documents that reflect Jefferson's view of political religious rights. Burstein says:

> If one looks at Jefferson's most notable public addresses, it is clear that he was careful to invoke the name of God, at least generally, in support of patriotic purposes he was at times sensi-

tive to the needs of his audience. He safely—cleverly, one might say—invoked the deistic "nature's god" in the Declaration of Independence. He concluded his first inaugural address with a prayer: "And may the Infinite Power which rules the destinies of the universe lead our councils to what is best." More tellingly, in his Bill for Establishing Religious Freedom, presented to the Virginia legislature, he opened with the dictum, "Almighty God hath created the mind free ..."[2]

Burstein provides further commentary:

> These few words summarize Jefferson's central presumption about a Creator God [that] did not force belief, and therefore it was absurd to believe that God could select any one ministry as the most righteous, or deserving of public support. It was simply a corruption of religion for civil authorities to grant a "monopoly of worldly honours and emoluments" to one church, or to connect civil rights to religious opinions at all, that was the tyranny Jefferson worried about. In the words of Priestly, church-state separation underpinned all politics. A civil magistrate should have no concern outside of his duty "to preserve the peace of society," and the church should concentrate on preparing people for "the life to come."[3]

In short, Thomas Jefferson was in favor of religious toleration and for the individual worship in any way he saw fit, while at the same time he was against the notion of an established church. These thoughts are repeated countless times in the documents mentioned above.

Among these documents are "rights which God and the laws have given equally to all."[4] The central premise of any of these documents was that God has created all people with a common intrinsic nature, as well as certain "natural rights." Jefferson's chief source for these political freedoms was John Locke, and his view that human beings are endowed with rights to life, liberty, and property.[5]

Jefferson sketched out some of these natural rights in his *Notes on the State of Virginia*. In this work, Jefferson expanded his idea of religious toleration at some length. To illustrate the error of not allowing religious toleration, Jefferson writes about the treatment of Galileo by the Roman church. In his *Commonplace Books*, Jefferson copied with enthusiasm Locke's line, "I cannot be saved by a worship I disbelieve and abhor."[6]

Jefferson was also among the first of the founding fathers to think and write about the separation of church and state. Again, in the *Notes on the State of Virginia*, Jefferson outlines his view that in Virginia the Anglican Church should not be seen as a state church. In Jefferson's *Autobiography*,[7] he again endorsed the same doctrine of separation, as he did in the *Act For Establishing Religious Freedom in Virginia*.[8] In this latter work, Jefferson makes seven different arguments for establishing religious freedom. Among those were: 1) Almighty God created the mind free, and willed that it shall remain free. 2) The use of corporal punishment or "civic incapacitations" to enforce uniform beliefs was doomed to failure. 3) It is sinful and tyrannical to force an individual to assent to a religion, "which he abhors and disbelieves." 4) It makes no more sense to penalize a man for his religious belief than it does to punish him for his views of science or education. 5) Religious establishment is wrong because it tends to corrupt the values of the institution it wishes to establish. 6) Truth and reason are greater than intolerance and will win in the end. And 7) Freedom of religion is one of man's natural rights. Any infringement of it is "an infringement of natural right."[9]

In countless places in the documents mentioned above, Jefferson regularly outlines his views of innate natural rights, religious toleration, the separation of church and state, and religious freedom. His general views of these matters have been accepted by most Jefferson scholars. In short, Jefferson was in favor of religious toleration and separation of church and state, while believing that humans were endowed with certain inalienable religious rights.

Daniel J. Boorstin sums up these political religious rights of Jefferson's view. He writes:

> Jefferson saw each man not in spiritual pursuit of the metaphysically accurate vision of the True God, but as engaging in an act of homage to his Creator. While it may have been impossible to make man's disparate theories of God logically consistent, the Jeffersonian had set himself quite another task, namely, to enable men sociably to perform their different acts of homage. There was no question of "consistency" here: problems arose only when a clash of opinions became a clash of men.[10]

Boorstin points out that this desire for what today would be called a multi-cultural religious heritage was shared by many of the other founding fathers as well, including John Adams and Thomas Paine. Paine wrote:

> Why may we not suppose that the great Father of all is pleased with a variety of devotion; and that the greatest offence we can act, is that by which we seek to torment and render each other miserable?

> ...I do not believe that any two men, on what are called doctrinal points, think alike who think at all. It is only those who have not thought that appear to agree.[11]

Jefferson's Idiosyncratic Religious Beliefs

In addition to these political religious beliefs, Jefferson also discusses a number of other religious and moral beliefs that he does not share with many. Among these is the view that religion is a private matter between oneself and one's God. Jefferson repeatedly voiced this opinion, mostly to his friends. In a letter to Mrs. Harrison Smith on August 6, 1816, Jefferson writes:

> But I have ever thought religion a concern purely between our God and our consciences, for which we are accountable to Him, and not to the priests.[12]

In a letter to the Danbury Baptists from January 1, 1802, Jefferson makes the same point:

> Believing with you that religion is a matter which lies solely between man and his God, that he owes account to none other for his faith or his worship, that the legislative powers of government reach actions only, and not opinions ...[13]

Again, in a letter to Miles King on September 26, 1814, Jefferson alludes to his belief about the privacy of religion:

> Our particular principals of religion are a subject of accountability to our God alone. I inquire after no man's, and trouble none

with mine; nor is it given to us in this life to know whether yours or mine, our friends or our foes, are exactly right.[14]

A second religious belief that Jefferson did not share with many people is his notion that the best judgment of religious views is the bar of reason. Eugene Sheridan writes about Jefferson's use of reason in religion:

> The rationalistic spirit that animated the Enlightenment inevitably brought it into conflict with organized Christianity, whose emphasis is on the value of supernatural revelation, tradition, and ecclesiastical authority was rejected by those who insisted that religion, like all other institutions, had to be justified on the twin grounds of reasonableness and social utility.[15]

In a letter to Timothy Pickering on February 27, 1821, Jefferson comments that "No one sees with greater pleasure than myself the progress of reason in its advances toward rational Christianity."[16]

In a number of his letters, Jefferson agrees with the use of these two grounds of justification. In a letter to Dr. Rush, Jefferson suggests that 'Every man's own reason must be his oracle.'[17] In the letter to his nephew Peter Carr cited many times in this work, Jefferson wrote:

> Your own reason is the only oracle given you by heaven, and you are answerable, not to the rightness, but uprightness of the decision.[18]

In a correspondence to Col. Nicholas Lewis on January 30, 1799, Jefferson also mentions the relation of religious belief to reason:

> Reason, not rashness, is the only means of bringing our fellow citizens to their true minds.[19]

"Reason and free inquiry are the only effectual agents against error,"[20] Jefferson wrote in his *Notes on the State of Virginia*. It is clear from these quotations, as well as numerous others that the final arbiter of religious disputes for our third president was the bar of reason.

A third belief that Jefferson appears to have shared with few others is his judgment that the human sense of morality is innate. In a letter to Thomas Law from June 13, 1814, Jefferson wrote:

> I sincerely, then, believe with you in the general existence of a
> moral instinct. I think it is the brightest gem with which the hu-
> man character is studded, and the want of it as more degrading
> than the most hideous of the bodily deformities.[21]

Jefferson believed this notion of a moral instinct was at the heart of
the good of the individual, as well as that of nations:

> We are firmly convinced, and we act on that conviction that with
> nations, as with individuals, our interests soundly calculated will
> ever be found inseparable from our moral duties.[22]

In a letter to James Fishback on September 27, 1809, Jefferson tells
us, that "God has taken care to impress its [morality's] precepts so indel-
ibly on our hearts . . ."[23] In the same letter, Jefferson writes to Fishback,
telling him that these moral precepts reside in the hearts of all men, and
in every society.

A final religious belief that is peculiar to Jefferson and few others
is his understanding that the natural world and its rhythms is a superior
way of gaining truth than the values of the individual or society. In this
regard, Jefferson speaks on numerous occasions of the values of farmers having a better understanding of the world than do people living in
cities. Jefferson also makes many comments about what can be learned
about the meaning of creation by examining items in the natural world.
In this letter to Thomas B. Parker, for example, written on May 15, 1819.
Jefferson tells us:

> Were I to be the founder of a new sect, I would call them
> Apiarians, and after the example of a bee, advise them to extract
> the honey of every sect. My fundamental principle would be the
> reverse of Calvin's, that we are to be saved by our good works
> which are within our power, and not by our faith which is not
> within our power.[24]

About farmers, Jefferson says this:

> Cultivators of the earth are the most valuable citizens. They are
> the most vigorous, the most independent, the most virtuous, and
> they are tied to their country, and wedded to its liberty, and inter-
> ests, by the most lasting bonds.[25]

Among the religious beliefs of Thomas Jefferson, then, are certain propositions that he seems to have shared with few other people. Chief among these are: that reason is the best judge of religion; that the sense of morality is innate; and that the natural world and the world of the farmer can tell us much about the way the world works.

This view of farmers being closer to God is expressed in a number of Jefferson's unpublished works, as well as in his *Notes on the State of Virginia*, like this comment about farmers in Query XIX:

> Those who labour in the earth are the chosen people of God, if ever He had a chosen people, whose breasts he has made his peculiar deposit for substantial and genuine virtue.[26]

Jefferson's Traditional Religious Beliefs

The third category of Jefferson's religious beliefs includes those propositions that Jefferson shares with orthodox Christianity. Chief among these beliefs are: that there is one and only one God; that God created the universe and all that is in it; and that Jesus was the greatest moral teacher and reformer of all time.

That Jefferson was a monotheist we have established in this work in a number of places. Jefferson often distinguishes his belief in one God with that of Calvin and others who believed in the Trinity and thus, in Jefferson's view, believed in three gods.

In a letter to Benjamin Waterhouse from June 26, 1822, mentioned earlier, Jefferson outlines his religious beliefs for his friend. The first of these is, "There is one only God, and He is all perfect."[27] Jefferson also discusses his belief that God created the universe in a number of places like, for example, in this letter to John Adams from April 11, 1823:

> Knowing how incomprehensible it was that a "word," the mere action or articulation of the organs of speech could create a world, they undertook to make of this articulation a second pre-existing being, and ascribe to him, and not to God, the creation of the universe.[28]

Jefferson also continuously refers to Jesus Christ as the greatest of moral teachers, something else he shares with traditional orthodox

Christianity. In a letter to Jared Sparks from November 4, 1820, Jefferson writes about Jesus as a moral teacher:

> I hold the precepts of Jesus as delivered by Himself, to be the most pure, benevolent, and sublime, which have ever been preached to man.[29]

In a letter to William Short on October 31, 1819, Jefferson refers to "The establishment of the innocent and genuine character of this benevolent Moralist [Jesus] ... "[30] For Jefferson, the life of Jesus was a morally exemplary one. And it is to Jesus' moral teachings we wish to turn in the next section of this chapter.

Jefferson's Moral Beliefs

We have argued several times in this work that the best way to understand Thomas Jefferson's view of Jesus, as well as Jefferson's moral vision, is carefully to look at those places in Jefferson's writings where he talks specifically about Jesus' moral teachings. For Jefferson, the whole of morality is to be summed up by referring to Jesus' treatment of moral matters. From Jefferson's gleaning of Jesus' moral teachings, our third president continuously refers to a whole set of moral beliefs that he got from the gospels. Chief among these beliefs is the golden rule: To do unto others as you would have them do to you. Jefferson makes hundreds of references to the teachings of Jesus. In addition to assenting to the golden rule, Jefferson also seems to agree with a number of Jesus' other moral teachings.

Among these teachings are the following: the cultivation of certain virtues leads to happiness; that one ought to be just, which Jefferson believes comes from virtue, which can only be found in the heart; work for peaceful resolutions to problems, even to the point of returning kindness to those who have been violent toward you; don't judge other people; don't hold grudges; be modest and unpretentious; give out of generosity, not for desire to be repaid; those who think they know the most are often the most ignorant; don't abide hypocrites; don't talk too much about righteousness; material riches don't constitute true wealth; the last shall be first and the first last; consider those things valuable that have no material value; and slavery is a "moral outrage."

In Jefferson's letters, his published works, and in his personal conversations as well, our third president often refers to these teachings. In Jefferson's view often the most interesting things about the gospels are the stories Jesus tells, and the morals we are supposed to derive from those tales. In Jefferson's view, there are no other moral teachings in the history of the human race to compare with those of Jesus Christ. As Jefferson wrote in a letter to William Canby on September 18, 1813:

> Of all the systems of morality, ancient or modern, which have come under my observation, none appear to be so pure as that of Jesus. He who follows this steadily need not, I think, be uneasy, although he cannot comprehend the subtleties and mysteries erected on his doctrines by those who, calling themselves his special followers and favorites, would make him come into the world to lay snares for all understanding but theirs.[31]

Jefferson also believed that these moral teachings of Jesus never lead to religious schism. Writing to Ezra Stiles on June 25, 1819, Jefferson tells us:

> No doctrine of His [Jesus] leads to schism. It is the speculation of crazy theologists which have made a Babel of religion the most moral and sublime ever preached to man, and calculated to heal, and not to create differences. These religious animosities I impute to those who call themselves His ministers, and who engraft their casuistries on the stock of His simple precepts. I am sometimes more angry with them than is authorized by the blessed charities which He preaches.[32]

Above all, Jefferson believed that the moral teachings of Jesus, as well as those of his own, are simple: In a correspondence to Dr. George Logan on October 3, 1813, Jefferson wrote:

> My principle is to do whatever is right, and leave consequences to Him who has the disposal of them.[33]

In a letter to Benjamin Waterhouse from June 26, 1822, Jefferson begins, "The doctrines of Jesus are simple, and tend to all the happiness of man."[34]

On other occasions, Jefferson wrote that the moral sense is nothing more than loving God, and following the Golden Rule. Indeed, Jefferson thought that the moral sense is instinctual and universal for all places and all times. Writing to John Adams on January 11, 1817, Jefferson said: "What all religions agree in morals is probably right. What no two agree in sectarian dogma, most probably wrong."[35]

Jefferson's Moral Advice

In addition to the moral precepts outlined above, Jefferson also gave much moral advice in his adult years. Much of that advice was given to his nephew, Peter Carr, but he also gave moral advice to a number of other people.

In a letter to his nephew Peter Carr on August 19, 1785, Jefferson outlines ten pieces of advice on how to deal with others. Jefferson writes:

1. Never put off till tomorrow what you can do today.

2. Never trouble another for what you can do yourself.

3. Never spend your money before you have it.

4. Never buy what you do not want, because it is cheap; it will be dear to you.

5. Pride cost us more than hunger, thirst, and cold.

6. We never repent of having eaten too little.

7. Nothing is troublesome that we do willingly.

8. How much pain has cost us the evils which have never happened.

9. Take things always by their smooth handle.

10. When angry, count ten, before you speak; if very angry, a hundred.[36]

On numerous other occasions, Jefferson also offers free moral advice. Again to Peter Carr on August 10, 1787, Jefferson tells his nephew, "Be good, be learned, and be industrious, and you will not want the aid of traveling, to render you precious to your country, dear to your friends, and happy within yourself."[37] In the same letter, Jefferson says to his nephew:

Above all things, lose no occasion of exercising your dispositions to be grateful, to be generous, to be charitable, to be humane, to be true, just, firm, orderly, courageous, etc. Consider every act of this kind, as an exercise which will strengthen your moral faculties and increase your worth.[38]

In a letter to John Adams on May 5, 1817, Jefferson even extends advice to the former president:

Men of energy and character must have enemies; because there are two sides to every question, and taking one with decision, and acting on it with effect, those who take the other will of course be hostile in proportion as they feel that effect.[39]

Jefferson was also among the first in America to give this advice:

Whenever you are to do a thing, though it can never be known but to yourself, ask yourself how you would act were all the world looking at you, and act accordingly.[40]

In a correspondence to his daughter Patsy from November 28, 1783, Jefferson gives his daughter a summation of his moral point of view:

If you love me then, strive to do good under every situation and to all living creatures, and to acquire those accomplishments which I have put in your power.[41]

Again, to his nephew Peter Carr, Jefferson gives sound advice about what to do when one finds oneself in a tough situation:

If you ever find yourself environed with difficulties and perplexing circumstances, out of which you are at a loss to extricate yourself, do what is right, and be assured that that will extricate you the best out of the worst situations. Though you cannot see, when you take one step, what will be the next, yet follow truth, justice, and plain dealing, and never fear their leading you out of the labyrinth, in the easiest manner possible. The knot which you thought a Gordian one, will untie itself before you.[42]

Jefferson had a prohibition against telling lies. He talks about it frequently when giving moral advice. In this letter to Peter Carr, Jefferson wrote:

> It is of great importance to set a resolution, not to be shaken,
> never to tell an untruth. There is no vice so mean, so pitiful, so
> contemptible; and he who permits himself to tell a lie once, finds
> it much easier to do it a second and third time, till at length it
> becomes habitual; he tells lies without attending to it, and truths
> without the world believing him. This falsehood of the tongue
> leads to that of the heart, and in time depraves all its good dis-
> positions.[43]

In summary, Jefferson often gave moral advice, to his nephew, to
his own children, and even to ex-president John Adams. Frequently, the
nature of that advice is to do the right thing. Jefferson believed each of
us knows the right thing because it is written by God on the hearts of
every human being. In Jefferson's view, human beings naturally have a
sense of morality.

Jefferson on Virtue

In addition to constructing a moral theory based on the teachings of
Jesus, Thomas Jefferson also admired a number of classical writers, and
their views of virtue. Among these writers were Epictetus, Epicurus, and
Cicero. In a letter to his nephew Peter Carr on August 10, 1787, in giving him advice about college, Jefferson advises his nephew that if there
is no God, then morality can be followed by a life devoted to virtue.
Jefferson says, "If it ends in a belief that there is no god, you will find in-
citement to virtue in the comfort and pleasantness you feel in its exercise,
and the love of others it will procure you."[44] In the same correspondence,
Jefferson continues on virtue:

> Above all, lose no occasion of exercising your dispositions to be
> grateful, to be generous, to be charitable, to be humane, to be true,
> just, firm, orderly, courageous, etc. Consider every act of faith of
> this kind, as an exercise that will strengthen your moral faculties,
> and increase your worth.[45]

In a number of his other writings, Jefferson, as well, outlines his view
of virtue. In a letter to William Short on October 31, 1819, Jefferson tells
us, "Epictetus and Epicurus give laws for governing themselves, Jesus a
supplement of the duties and charities we owe to others."[46] In the same

letter to Short, Jefferson enumerates the virtues in something he calls, "A Syllabus on the Doctrines of Epicurus." Jefferson writes:

> Virtue is the foundation of morality. Utility the test for virtue . . .
> Virtue consists in 1. Prudence, 2. Temperance, 3. Fortitude, 4.
> Justice.[47]

In another letter to Peter Carr on August 19, 1785, Jefferson again writes about virtue:

> From the practice of the purest virtue, you may be assured you
> will derive the most sublime comforts in every moment of life,
> and in the moment of death.[48]

In the same letter, Jefferson advises his nephew:

> Encourage all your virtuous dispositions, and exercise them
> whenever an opportunity arises; being assured that they will gain
> strength by exercise, as a limb of the body does, and that exercise
> will make them habitual.[49]

Jefferson seems here to adopt an Aristotelean conception of virtue that suggests virtue and vice become habitual parts of character. Jefferson also alludes to this theory of virtue in a letter to Robert Skipwith on August 3, 1771:

> Everything is useful which contributes to fix us in the principles
> and practice of virtue.[50]

In this same letter, Jefferson also suggests the view of Aristotle about virtue being habitual:

> Now every emotion of this kind is an exercise of our virtuous
> dispositions; and dispositions of the mind, like limbs of the body,
> acquire strength by exercise. But exercise produces habit; and in
> the instance of which we speak, the exercise being of the moral
> feelings, produces a habit of thinking and acting virtuously.[51]

In a letter to Amos Cook on January 21, 1816, Jefferson again seems to allude to an Aristotelean sense of virtue and its relationship to happiness. Jefferson tells Cook, "If the Wise be the happy man, as these sages say, he must be virtuous too; for without virtue, happiness cannot be."[52]

Jefferson sums up his view of virtue in this correspondence to William Short on October 31, 1819:

> As you say of yourself, I too am an Epicurean. I consider the genuine (not the imputed) doctrines of Epicurus as containing everything rational in moral philosophy which Greece and Rome have left us. Epictetus indeed, has given us what was good of the Stoics; and beyond, of their dogmas, being hypocrisy and grimace.[53]

Jefferson believed the Stoics' moral theory was the best thing that came out of Roman philosophy, and that the Epicurean view of virtue was among the greatest of Greek moral teachings, as well.

Although Jefferson held an Aristotelean view of virtue, at times he held that the purposes for acquiring a life of virtue were utilitarian:

> Some have argued against the existence of a moral sense, by saying that if nature had given us such a sense ... then nature would also have designated, by some particular ear-marks, the two sets of actions, which are, in themselves, the one virtuous and the other vicious. Whereas, we find, in fact, that the same actions are deemed virtuous in one country and vicious in another. The answer is that nature has constituted *utility* to man, the standard and test of virtue. Men living in different countries, under different circumstances, different habits and regimens, may have different utilities.[54]

One final moral belief of Thomas Jefferson is related to our third president's views of slavery. Although Jefferson kept slaves his entire life, nevertheless, there is ample evidence that Thomas Jefferson thought that slavery was inherently evil. This conclusion comes principally from three sources. First, comments made on slavery in his published works. Chief among these are his *Notes on the State of Virginia*, the *Articles of Confederation*, and the first draft of the *Declaration of Independence*. The second source of materials on Jefferson's view of slavery is his actions in regard to slavery while he was president. The third source for Jefferson's view of slavery is in a number of letters where he writes specifically about his understanding of slavery. In all three of these sources, Jefferson arrives at the same conclusion: that slavery is inherently evil, and that its practice is morally wrong.

In a number of places in his *Notes on the State of Virginia,* Thomas Jefferson refers to slavery. Queries XIV, XVII, and XVIII contain a number of observations about slavery. In Query XIV, Jefferson suggests that "slaves, as well as land, were entailable during the monarchy." But then he goes on to suggest it ought to be abolished in the colonies.[55] Later in Query XIV, Jefferson speaks of "deep rooted prejudices entertained by the whites, and ten thousand recollections by the blacks, of the injuries they have sustained."[56] Jefferson also discusses Greek and Roman practices of slavery in Query XIV, and he points out that, unlike America, both slaves and masters were white in the Greco-Roman world.[57] In Query XVIII, Jefferson discusses slavery in the context of manners. Jefferson writes there, "The whole commerce between master and slave is a perpetual exercise of the most boisterous passions, the most unremitting despotism."[58]

Jefferson also mentions slavery in the *Articles of Confederation.* It is mostly about how to determine the worth of slaves. He discusses several proposals offered by Samuel Chase, John Adams, Benjamin Harrison, James Wilson, Theodore Payne, and John Witherspoon. Chase had offered an amendment to the *Articles* that called for a colony's population to be judged by the number of white inhabitants. The amendment was defeated. Jefferson was in favor of the suggestion of Mr. Payne who argued that population should be determined by the "number of souls" in a particular colony.[59]

In addition to these remarks on slavery in the *Articles of Federation* and in *Notes on the State of Virginia,* Jefferson also introduced a clause in the first draft of the *Declaration of Independence* that condemned the slave trade as a "moral outrage."[60] He also prevented slavery from being extended to the Northwest Territory, and as president, Jefferson got Congress to abolish the slave trade, and to prohibit any further importing of slaves to the United States.

In addition to the evidence mentioned above, Jefferson also mentions his views of slavery in his *Autobiography* and in a number of his private letters. In his *Autobiography,* Jefferson called slavery an "abomination." In a letter to Jean Nicholas Demeunier, Jefferson suggests he and Mr. Wythe were in favor of the emancipation of slaves.[61] In a letter to Francois Jean Chastellux from June 17, 1785, Jefferson argues against the notion that slaves in America are inferior to the lower classes in Europe.[62]

In a letter to Benjamin Banneker from August 30, 1791, Jefferson begins this way:

> Sir:
>
> I thank you sincerely for your letter of the 19th instant and for the almanac it contained. No body wishes more than I do to see such proofs as you exhibit, that nature has given to our black brethren, talents equal to those of the other colors of men, and that the appearance of a want of them is owing merely to the degraded condition of their existence, both in Africa and America.[63]

Jefferson makes similar remarks in correspondences to James Monroe on November 24, 1801, and to Henri Gregoire, where he writes:

> Sir:
>
> I have received the favor of your letter of August 17th, and with it the volume you were so kind to send me on the "Literature of Negroes." Be assured that no person living wishes more sincerely than I do, to see a complete refutation of the doubts I have myself entertained and expressed on the grade of understanding allotted to them by nature, and to find in this respect, they are on a par with ourselves.[64]

In his private correspondence, Jefferson repeatedly refers to his beliefs that blacks are equal to whites, that slavery is an abomination, and that all slaves in America should be emancipated. In a letter to Edward Coles on August 25, 1814, Jefferson speaks of emancipation:

> Sir:
>
> Your favor of July 31, was duly received, and was read with peculiar pleasure. The sentiments breathed through the whole do honor to both the head and heart of the writer. Mine on the subject of slavery of negroes have long since been in possession of the public, and time has only served to give them stronger root. The love of justice and the love of country plead equally the cause of these people, and it is a moral reproach to us that they should have pleaded it so long, in vain.[65]

To Albert Gallatin on December 26, 1820, Jefferson again refers to his desire for emancipation. He writes:

> ... Amidst this prospect of evil, I am glad to see one good effect. It has brought the necessity of some plan of general emancipation and deportation more home to the minds of our people than it has ever been before.[66]

From this evidence, it should be clear that Jefferson was in favor of emancipation of slaves, and believed that blacks were not inferior to whites long before his death in 1826. There is no evidence that Jefferson ever believed anything about slavery other than that it is inherently, morally wrong.

Indeed, one of the last letters written by Thomas Jefferson was to James Heaton, who had inquired of Jefferson the president's view of slavery. He replies to Heaton's letter on May 20, 1826:

> Dear Sir:
>
> The subject of your letter of April 20th, is one on which I do not permit myself an opinion, but when time, place, and occasion may give it some favorable effect. A good cause is often injured more by ill-timed effects of its friend than by the arguments of its enemies. Persuasion, perseverance, and patience are the best advocates on questions depending on the will of others. The revolution of public opinion which this cause requires, is not to be expected in a day, or perhaps in an age; but time, which outlives all things, will outlive this evil also. My sentiments have been forty years before the public. Had I repeated them forty times, they would only become the more stale and threadbare. Although I shall not live to see them consummated, they will not die with me; but living or dying, they will ever be in my most fervent prayer. This is written for yourself and not for the public, in compliance with your request of two lines of sentiment on the subject. Accept the assurance of my good will and respect.
>
> Thomas Jefferson[67]

From the materials discussed above, we may make three general conclusions about Jefferson's view of race. First, in his entire adult life, Jefferson saw slavery as an abomination, a "moral outrage" as he called it in the first draft of the Constitution. Secondly, Jefferson believed that blacks were not inferior to people of the white race, and that blacks were endowed with the same rights as white people. And finally, from very early on, and throughout his adult life, Jefferson was in favor of the emancipation of slaves.

Beyond this evidence that Jefferson believed that slavery was a moral abomination, and that he held this view throughout his entire life, is another more fundamental question. Should we hold Thomas Jefferson by the moral standards of his age, or by contemporary moral sensibilities? In Jefferson's day, and in his social class, most white men owned slaves. It was, for the day, a morally acceptable practice. Judging him by contemporary western rules of morality seems unfair. If we judge Jefferson by contemporary standards must we not do the same for Plato, Aristotle, Augustine, Thomas Aquinas, and others on their views on race and gender? If that is what we ought to do, then how could any of these men in their own times really know what the moral good is? More importantly, how do we know that two hundred years from now our moral sensibilities might not be so different from what we believe now? It could be the case that in a few hundred years we will find out that even our modern moral sensibilities are subject to change. This process could continue in an infinite regress, where it is impossible to make any moral judgments about race and gender.

Throughout his adult life, Thomas Jefferson was reticent to express his views about race; but privately, in his letters and conversations he expressed a conviction that he believed in the equality of black Americans. As he wrote in one letter:

> That no person living wishes more sincerely than I do, to see a complete refutation of the doubts I have myself entertained and expressed on the grade of understanding allotted to them by nature and to find that in this respect they are on a par with ourselves.[68]

The bottom line on Thomas Jefferson's view of slavery is that he believed that all people were created equal and endowed with certain moral rights. He held that view early on, and he continued to hold it for over forty years, until his death in 1826. It makes little sense to hold Jefferson to standards that did not exist until two hundred years after his time.

Conclusions

In this chapter, we have attempted to present an outline of Thomas Jefferson's most important moral and religious beliefs. We have suggested that Jefferson's beliefs with respect to these matters can be divided into five types; beliefs about political rights; beliefs that are peculiar to Jefferson and perhaps a few others; beliefs that Jefferson shares with traditional Christianity; beliefs related to Jesus' moral teachings; and beliefs that Jefferson held when dispensing moral advice.

We shall end this chapter, and this study as well, with a review of those religious and moral beliefs to which Thomas Jefferson assented.

A) Jefferson's Political Beliefs related to Religion.

    1 We are endowed by our Creator with natural religious rights.

    2 Among our natural rights is the right of religious freedom.

    3 Religious toleration should be practiced for all.

    4 There should be no established church, and a separation of church and state.

B) Religious Beliefs peculiar to Jefferson and a few others.

    5 Religion ought to be a private matter between one's God and oneself.

    6 The best judge for evaluating religious beliefs should be reason.

    7 The sense of morality is innate and universal.

    8 The rhythms of the natural world are a good source for truth.

C) Jefferson's Traditional Christian Beliefs

    9 There is only one God.

    10 God created the universe out of nothing.

    11 Jesus Christ is the greatest of moral teachers.

D) Jefferson's Moral Beliefs

12 The cultivation of certain values leads to happiness.

13 Follow the Golden Rule.

14 Be Just.

15 Virtue is habitual and to be found in the heart.

16 Work for peaceful resolutions to problems.

17 Respond with kindness and compassion to violence.

18 Don't judge others.

19 Don't bear grudges.

20 Be modest and unpretentious.

21 Be generous.

22 Don't abide hypocrites.

23 Tell the truth.

24 Don't assume material riches constitute wealth.

25 Consider those things valuable that have no material value.

26 Slavery is a "moral outrage."

These twenty-six propositions were beliefs to which Thomas Jefferson regularly assented; and these beliefs were also the core of the moral advice that Jefferson often gave to the young. One can conclude this work by saying that Jefferson was not an atheist. He never announced in his public writings or speeches that he was a Deist or Unitarian, though he certainly shared beliefs with both groups. And finally, Jefferson considered himself a Christian, only in so far as he was a follower of the moral teachings of Jesus Christ. It is only fitting to give Jefferson the last word in this study.

> Christ has said, "wheresoever two or three are gathered together in his name, He will be in the midst of them." This is the definition of society. He does not make it essential that a bishop or presbyter govern them. Without them, it suffices for the salvation of souls.[69]

Notes

1. Henry Stephens Randall, *The Life of Thomas Jefferson*, Three Volumes (New York, 1858) Volume III, 555.

2. Andrew Burstein, *Jefferson's Secrets: Death and Desire and Monticello* (New York: Basic, 2005) 248.

3. Ibid.

4. Thomas Jefferson, *Notes on the State of Virginia*.

5. John Locke, *An Essay Concerning Human Understanding* (New York: Hackett, 1996) 196.

6. Thomas Jefferson, *Commonplace Books*.

7. Thomas Jefferson, *Autobiography*.

8. Thomas Jefferson, *An Act For Establishing Religious Freedom in Virginia*.

9. Ibid.

10. Daniel J. Boorstin, *The Lost World of Thomas Jefferson* (Chicago: University of Chicago Press, 1994) 123.

11. Thomas Paine, *The Rights of Man* Quoted in John Keane, *Tom Paine: A Political Life* (Boston, 1995) 430.

12. Thomas Jefferson, Letter to Mrs. Harrison Smith, August 6, 1816.

13. Thomas Jefferson, Letter to Danbury Baptists, January 1, 1802.

14. Thomas Jefferson, Letter to Miles King, September 26, 1814.

15. Sheridan, 14–15.

16. Thomas Jefferson, Letter to Timothy Pickering, February 27, 1821.

17. Thomas Jefferson, Letter to Benjamin Rush, March 6, 1813.

18. Thomas Jefferson, Letter to Peter Carr, August 10, 1787.

19. Thomas Jefferson to Nicholas Lewis, January 30, 1799.

20. Thomas Jefferson, *Notes on the State of Virginia*.

21. Thomas Jefferson, Letter to Thomas Law, June 13, 1814.

22. Ibid.

23. Thomas Jefferson, Letter to James Fishback, September 27, 1809.

24. Thomas Jefferson, Letter to Thomas B. Parker, May 15, 1819.

25. Thomas Jefferson, *Notes on the State of Virginia*.

26. Thomas Jefferson, *Notes on the State of Virginia* (Chapel Hill: W.W. Norton, 1954) 164–65.

27. Thomas Jefferson, Letter to Benjamin Waterhouse, June 26, 1822.

28. Thomas Jefferson, Letter to John Adams, April 11, 1823.

29. Thomas Jefferson, Letter to Jared Sparks, November 4, 1820.

30. Thomas Jefferson, Letter to William Short, October 31, 1819.

31. Thomas Jefferson, Letter to William Canby, September 18, 1813.

32. Thomas Jefferson, Letter to Ezra Stiles, June 25, 1819.

33. Thomas Jefferson, Letter to George Logan, October 3, 1813.

34. Thomas Jefferson, Letter to Benjamin Waterhouse, June 26, 1822.

35. Thomas Jefferson, Letter to John Adams, January 11, 1817.

36. Thomas Jefferson to Peter Carr, August 19, 1785.

37. Thomas Jefferson to Peter Carr, August 10, 1787.

38. Ibid.

39. Thomas Jefferson, Letter to John Adams, May 5, 1817.

40. Thomas Jefferson, Letter to Peter Carr, August 19, 1785.

41. Thomas Jefferson, Letter to Patsy Jefferson, November 28, 1783.

42. Thomas Jefferson, Letter to Peter Carr, August 10, 1787.

43. Thomas Jefferson, Letter to Peter Carr, August 19, 1785.

44. Thomas Jefferson, Letter to Elbridge Gerry, March 29, 1801.

45. Thomas Jefferson, Letter to Peter Carr, August 10, 1787.

46. Ibid.

47. Thomas Jefferson, Letter to William Short, October 31, 1819.

48. Ibid.

49. Thomas Jefferson, Letter to Peter Carr, August 19, 1785.

50. Ibid.

51. Thomas Jefferson, Letter to Robert Skipwith, August 3, 1771.

52. Thomas Jefferson, Letter to Amos Cook, January 21, 1816.

53. Ibid.

54. Thomas Jefferson, "Essay on Education," in *Lectures on History* in *The Works of Thomas Jefferson*, edited by Paul Leicester Ford (12 volumes, Federal ed; New York: 1907) Volume 7, xxxv.

55. Thomas Jefferson, *Notes on the State of Virginia*, Query XIV.

56. Ibid.

57. Ibid.

58. Ibid. Query XVIII.

59. Thomas Jefferson, *Articles of Confederation* in *Jefferson's Writings* (New York: Library of America, 1984) 24–31.

60. Thomas Jefferson, *Declaration of Independence*, First Draft.

61. Thomas Jefferson, Letter to Jean Nicolas Demeunier, June 26, 1786.

62. Thomas Jefferson, Letter to Francois Jean Chastellux, June 7, 1785.

63. Thomas Jefferson, Letter to Benjamin Banneker, August 30, 1791.

64. Thomas Jefferson, Letter to Henri Gregoire, November 24, 1801.

65. Thomas Jefferson, Letter to Edward Coles, August 25, 1814.

66. Thomas Jefferson, Letter to Albert Gallatin, December 26, 1820.

67. Thomas Jefferson, Letter to James Heaton, May 20, 1826.

Select Bibliography

Abbott, John S. C. *Lives of the Presidents*. Portland, ME: Hallett, 1890.

Allen, Ethan. *Reason the Only Oracle of Man*. New York: Burt Franklin, 1972.

George Bancroft, *A History of the United States*. Bostson: Little, Brown, 1834.

Bernstein, R. B. *Thomas Jefferson*. New York: Oxford University Press, 2003.

Boller, Paul F. *George Washington and Religion*. Dallas: SMU Press, 1963.

Byrne, James M. *Religion and the Enlightenment: From Descartes to Kant*. Louisville: Westminster John Knox, 1997.

Byrne, Peter. *Natural Religion and the Nature of Religion: The Legacy of Deism*. London: Routledge, 1989.

Chinard, Gilbert. *Thomas Jefferson: The Apostle of Americanism*. Ann Arbor: University of Michigan Press, 1957.

Chubb, Thomas. *The Supremacy of the Father Asserted*. London: Roberts, 1715.

Dwight, Timothy. *A Discourse on Some Events of the Last Century: Delivered in the Brick Church in New Haven on Wednesday, January 7, 1801*. New Haven, 1801.

Ellis, Joseph J. *American Sphinx: The Character of Thomas Jefferson*. New York: Vintage Books, 1996.

Emerson, Ralph Waldo. "Nature." In *Selected Essays* (New York: Penguin Books, 1982).

———. "Self Reliance." In *Essays and Lectures*. New York: Library of America, 2005.

Gaustad, Edwin S. *Sworn on the Altar of God: A Religious Biography of Thomas Jefferson*. Grand Rapids: Eerdmans, 1996.

Gould, William D. "The Religious Opinions of Thomas Jefferson," *Mississippi Valley Historical Review* 20 (1933) 191–208.

Hall, Leslie. "The Religious Opinions of Thomas Jefferson." *Sewanee Review* 21 (1913) 163–76.

Hamburger, Philip. *Separation of Church and State*. Cambridge: Harvard University Press, 2002.

Hitchens, Christopher. *Thomas Jefferson: Author of America*. New York: HarperCollins, 2005.

Haakonssen, Knud. *Enlightenment and Religion: Rational Dissent in Eighteenth-Century Britain* (Cambridge: Cambridge University Press, 1996).

Jayne, Allen. *The Religious and Moral Wisdom of Thomas Jefferson: An Anthology*. New York: Vantage, 1984.

Jefferson, Thomas. *Basic Writings of Thomas Jefferson*. Edited by Philip S. Foner. New York: Willey, 1944.

———. *The Commonplace Book of Thomas Jefferson*. Edited by Gilbert Chinard. Baltimore: Johns Hopkins University Press, 1926.

———. *The Life and Morals of Jesus of Nazareth / Extracted Textually from the Gospels in Greek, Latin, French, and English by Thomas Jefferson; with an Introduction.* Washington: Government Printing Office, 1904.

———. *Papers.* Edited by Julian Boyd. Princeton: Princeton University Press, 1950–.

———. *The Writings of Thomas Jefferson.* Edited by Albert Ellery Bergh. Washington D.C., 1904–1905.

———. *The Writings of Thomas Jefferson.* Edited by Paul Leicester Ford. 10 vols. New York: Putnam, 1892–1899.

Locke, John. *The Reasonableness of Christianity.* Oxford: Clarendon, 1999.

———. *An Essay Concerning Human Understanding.* Edited by Kenneth P. Winkler. New York: Hackett Books, 1996.

Lodge, Henry C. *The Works of Alexander Hamilton.* New York: Putnam, 1904.

Madison, James. *The Papers of James Madison.* Edited by William Hutchinson et al. Vol. 12. Charlottesville: University of Virginia Press, 1979.

Malone, Dumas. *Jefferson and the Rights of Man.* 1951. Reprint, Charlottesville: University of Virginia Press, 2005.

Middleton, Conyers. *Introductory Discourse and the Free Inquiry.* London, 1757.

Padover, Saul K. *Jefferson: A Great American's Life and Ideas.* New York: Mentor Books, 1964.

Paine, Thomas. *The Age of Reason.* Mineola, NY: Dover, 2004.

Parker, Theodore. *A Discourse on the Transient and Permanent in Christianity.* Boston: Freeman and Bolles, 1841.

Priestly, Joseph. *Joseph Priestly: Selections from His Writings.* Edited by Ira V. Brown. University Park: Pennsylvania State University Press, 1962.

Randall, Henry Stephens. *The Life of Thomas Jefferson.* New York: Derby and Jackson, 1858.

Remsburg, John E. *Six Historic Americans.* New York: Truth Seeker, 1906.

Sacks, Kenneth S. *Understanding Emerson: "The American Scholar" and His Struggle for Self-Reliance.* Princeton: Princeton University Press, 2003.

Sanford, Charles B. *The Religious Life of Thomas Jefferson.* Charlottesville: University Press of Virginia, 1984.

Schultz, Constance Barlett. "The Radical Religious Ideas of Thomas Jefferson and John Adams: A Comparison." Ph.D. Dissertation, University of Cincinnati, 1973.

Sheridan, Eugene R. *Jefferson and Religion.* Charlottesville: Thomas Jefferson Memorial Foundation, 1998.

Swedenborg, Emanuel. *The Gist of Swedenborg.* Compiled by Julian K. Smyth and William F. Wunsch. Philadelphia: Lippincott, 1920.

———. *Heavenly Secrets.* Westchester, PA: Swedenborg Foundation, 1998.

———. *The True Christian Religion.* Westchester, PA: Swedenborg Foundation, 1996.

Tafel, J. F. I. *Documents Concerning the Life and Character of Emanuel Swedenborg.* Westchester, PA: Swedenborg Foundation, 1857–1877.

Thoreau, Henry David. *Walden.* New York: Houghton Mifflin, 2004.

Toland, John. *Christianity Not Mysterious.* London: Thoemmes Continuum, 1999.

Wilson, Douglas L. *Jefferson's Books.* Charlottesville: Monticello Foundation, 2002.

Index